D1512274

A New Owner's
Guide to
DALMATIANS

JG-105

The Publisher wishes to acknowledge the following owners of the dogs in this book: Janet Ashbey, Janey Baughn, Ely and Susan Bernstein, Susan E. Bloom, Andrea Boyce, Anne and Robert Carpenter, Joan Clancy, Coach Chase Dalmatians, Dynasty Dalmatians, Karen Ganly, Susan George, Gerald E. Hastings, Charlotte Katz, Judy Kristoff, Dana Lovett, Pauline L. Masaschi, Jean H. Meader, Jim and Marie Mercready, Dave and Carol Moran, Ellen Murray, John Murphy, S. &. K. Panka, Sharron Podleski, Deirde and Timothy Rahn, Judith Ann Reilly, Mrs. Alan Robson, Helen W. Shue, Maryann and Sherry Slonaker, Chin Nyok Soo, and Jack Sutton.

Photographers: John Ashbey, Paulette Braun, Bob Carpenter, Isabelle Francais, Robert Pearcy, Ron Reagan, Robert Smith, and Karen Taylor. Original art by John Quinn.

The author acknowledges the contribution of Judy Iby for the following chapters: Sport of Purebred Dogs, Identification and Finding the Lost Dog, Traveling with Your Dog, and Health Care for Your Dog.

Title page: The choice of many dog owners, Dalmatians can fit into the active lifestyle of any owner up to the challenge of these handsome and vigorous dogs.

Distributed in the UNITED STATES to the Pet Trade by T.F.H. Publications, Inc., One T.F.H. Plaza, Neptune City, NJ 07753; distributed in the UNITED STATES to the Bookstore and Library Trade by National Book Network, Inc. 4720 Boston Way, Lanham MD 20706; in CANADA to the Pet Trade by H & L Pet Supplies Inc., 27 Kingston Crescent, Kitchener, Ontario N2B 2T6; Rolf C. Hagen Inc., 3225 Sartelon St. Laurent-Montreal Quebec H4R 1E8; in CANADA to the Book Trade by Vanwell Publishing Ltd., 1 Northrup Crescent, St. Catharines, Ontario L2M 6P5 ; in ENGLAND by T.F.H. Publications, PO Box 15, Waterlooville PO7 6BQ; in AUSTRALIA AND THE SOUTH PACIFIC by T.F.H. (Australia), Pty. Ltd., Box 149, Brookvale 2100 N.S.W., Australia; in NEW ZEALAND by Brooklands Aquarium Ltd. 5 McGiven Drive, New Plymouth, RD1 New Zealand; in Japan by T.F.H. Publications, Japan—Jiro Tsuda, 10-12-3 Ohjidai, Sakura, Chiba 285, Japan; in SOUTH AFRICA by Lopis (Pty) Ltd., P.O. Box 39127, Booysens, 2016, Johannesburg, South Africa. Published by T.F.H. Publications, Inc.
MANUFACTURED IN THE
UNITED STATES OF AMERICA
BY T.F.H. PUBLICATIONS, INC.

A New Owner's Guide to
Guide to
DALMATIANS

Helen W. Shue

Contents

Litter of Dal pups in exercise pen.

The Dalmatian as the original "coach" dog.

Spotting the perfect Dal puppy is no easy task.

Nylabones® are safe chewing pacifiers for your Dalmatian.

Your Dalmatian will benefit from regular exercise.

FOREWORD

There is no question that the Dalmatian has gained increased popularity in the past decade. The entries at dog shows have doubled, the number of specialty shows has increased, and the number of local clubs is also on the rise.

The release of the Walt Disney movie *101 Dalmatians* onto home video has also helped to increase the popularity of the Dalmatian as a family pet. Today you cannot go into any store without seeing a Dalmatian on clothes, towels, toys and housewares.

The steady rise of popularity of the Dalmatian, both as a companion dog and as a show dog, makes it ever so important for potential buyers of the breed to understand all they can on the raising and training of the Dalmatian.

THE DALMATIAN

Of all the breeds of dogs I see
Just one spotted fellow appeals to me.
There are many kinds of dogs in our nation
To me, there is just one, the Dalmatian.

A Dalmatian's spots make it unique to the dog world. There is no mistaking a Dalmatian for any other breed, not even when it is a puppy.

Bold black spots on a field of
  white,
That field of white so sparkling
  bright,
Two eyes so filled with love for
  man,
A heart that serves your every
  plan.
The size is right for one and all,
Not too short, not too tall.
Happy when you're smiling,
Droopy when you're sad.
So, once you have owned a Dal,
You'll say there is no finer pal.
He'll stick with you through thick
  or thin,
A friend to please your every
  whim.

Lois J. Thiesen
The Spotter, June 1967

Yes, all Dalmatians are spotted, but just like human fingerprints no two Dals are spotted alike.

The devotion a Dalmatian displays for his owner can easily be seen in its facial expression.

ORIGIN and History of the Dalmatian

The Dalmatian, or carriage dog, is an ancient breed that has come down to us through the centuries unchanged. Its origin has always been a mystery. No other breed has a more interesting or more disputed heritage than the Dalmatian. Though the breed has been accredited with at least a half dozen nationalities, and as many native names, there is no definitive proof that any one country can call itself the homeland of the Dalmatian.

Mrs. Hebe Bedwell owned a print showing a Dalmatian-type dog with excellent spotting running alongside a war chariot, probably Egyptian or Babylonian in origin. Other paintings and models of antiquity show him in other Egyptian or Roman settings, proving that the "Spotted Dog" goes far back in the history of mankind.

However, we must accept the premise that nothing with any certainty is known about the origin of the Dalmatian. The name would suggest it originated in Dalmatia, a coastal region of Yugoslavia, but the name Dalmatian doesn't seem to appear until the end of the 18th century. It is also believed that the Dalmatian was used as a sentinel and dog of war on the borders of Dalmatia and Croatia.

Although no longer used to run alongside carriages, the Dalmatian, or "Coach Dog," is still commonly known as the firehouse mascot.

Spotted dogs were also known in France. A picture of the Dauphin of France (1655-1732) shows his highness petting a spotted dog very similar in type to the present-day Dalmatian. There is also a German painting that was done in the latter part of the 16th century in which the painter Herr F. Castiglione depicted two very typical Dalmatian-type dogs, proving that the Dalmatian was known throughout various countries.

All those who encounter the Dalmatian immediately become enamored of this regal and agile spotted dog.

It was the English that first gave the Dalmatian its great popularity. It is thought that the breed was brought to the country by gypsies and used in minstrel shows as performers and guard dogs for the wandering troops. The Dalmatian was admired and loved by all who saw this regal and agile spotted dog.

Their affinity for horses soon led them to their well-known name "Coach Dog" or "Carriage Dog." Their ability and agility to run between the carriage wheels and the horses hoofs and their stamina to run great distances made them ideal for traveling long and far with a coach.

They guided the horses through the streets and guarded the occupants of the coach against the notorious highwaymen.

This ability to run with horse and carriage is the reason the Dalmatian was so widely used with the fire carriage of yesteryear. They would carefully and aptly guide the fireman through the streets of busy traffic. Today, with no horse-drawn carriages for fire trucks, the Dalmatian has become the firehouse mascot. Contrary to popular belief, the Dalmatian was not used because he could see through smoke or because he liked the color red, but because he was a useful tool in guiding the carriages.

Dalmatian pups are born all white with visible pigment spots in the skin. These quickly darken with age.

There are all sorts of legends associated with the origin of this beautiful spotted breed and the one that

is most fascinating derives its origin from England. The Dalmatian is born pure white, like a piece of satin. The story holds that the wealthy aristocrats did away with many a newborn pup, fearing that their beautiful bitch had been entangled with a renegade mutt. Fortunately, someone realized that the spotting of these dogs comes later in their development, or who can say what might have become of the Spotted Dog?

When the Dalmatian first came to America is not known. We do know that during the Revolutionary War George Washington, in one of his letters, inquires into the possibility of acquiring a Dalmatian stud dog for his bitches.

The first recorded registration in the American Kennel Club Stud Book was in the 1880s of a dog named Bessie. The registration was as follows: *Bessie 10519 (Bitch); Mrs. N.L. Harvey, San Francisco, Cal. Whelped October 1887; white, black, tan. Breeder and pedigree unknown. Bench show 2nd, San Francisco, 1888.*

Afterwards registrations of Dalmatians were very few. However, there may have been a large number of purebred dogs that were never registered in the Stud Book, as registration of parents was unnecessary in those days. In 1899, we find one Dalmatian register, a bitch, owned by Joseph Thomas, Jr. of New York

Many champion Dalmatians of today can be traced back to show dogs of the early era.

In 1905, the size of the Stud Book doubled and we now find nine dogs and six bitches registered that year. These Dalmatians were primarily from the kennels of Windy Valley and Rockcliffe. In 1917, the Stud Book listed 50 Dalmatian Champions of Record, with Windholmes and Rockcliffe Kennels in the lead. From 1917 until 1939 the registration of Dalmatians decreased, but by January of 1941, the registration of Dals increased by leaps and bounds and has continued to do so in today's registration records. Several kennel names that appear in these early Stud Books can still be found in pedigrees of today.

Early kennel names that appear on almost all pedigrees of show dogs of the early era are Roadcoach, Four In Hand, and Tally Ho. Some more recent important kennel names are Green Star, Dal Quest, Coachman, Tuckaway, and Dalmatia. Ch. Lucky James and Ch. Venus of the Wells, both from Great Britain and owned by Miss E. V. Wells, were behind many imports to the United States and various countries. Ch. Lord

This nicely spotted pup is about fifty generations after Bessie.

Jim, Ch. Roadcoach Roadster, Ch. Four In Hand Mischief, and Ch. Green Star's Colonel Joe were some of the greatest Dalmatians in the history of the breed in the United States.

Not until the turn of the century were Dalmatian classes offered at shows. This is Ch. Lyco's Homecoming Queen owned by the author, Helen W. Shue.

It was near the turn of the century that the first Dalmatian classes were offered at dog shows. Today, the Dalmatian classes are one of the largest, with many specialty shows shown all over the country and Canada.

The Dalmatian Club of America, or the parent club as it is known, is of extreme importance to people who are interested in showing their dog, entering in obedience training, or eventually breeding their bitch. There is great knowledge to be gained from the people who belong to such clubs, both formally and informally, if only to learn more about the breed.

The Dalmatian Club of America was founded in 1904 and admitted as an associated member of the American Kennel Club in 1905. There were originally 26 members of the club. Alfred Maclay was the first president, Harry T. Peters was the vice-president, and Sergeant Price, Jr. was the secretary/treasurer.

The club was formed to promote and advance the quality of the breeding, care, training and exhibition of the breed. Its responsibilities included disseminating information concerning the breed, defining the standard, holding dog shows and other exhibitions, and promoting research into the breeding and care of the Dalmatian. At the club's formation, they adopted the 1890 Dalmatian standard with slight variations from the English Kennel Club.

There are many local as well as national clubs that Dal owners can join to enjoy the popularity of their breed as well as socialize their Dals with others of their kind.

Today the publication *The Spotter* is the official Dalmatian Club of America's quarterly magazine. It features articles on research and the care and training of the Dalmatian as well as pictures of many of the current winning show dogs.

Today, Dalmatian clubs are present

all over the United States and in various other countries. There is a special bond between all clubs and club members. This is due not only to a shared love of the breed, but also a commitment to improve breeding practices and the overall quality of the Dalmatian.

The Dalmatian is a very strong and agile breed that requires daily exercise. Even as a puppy, there is nothing more pleasing to the eye than a Dalmatian running free.

Today's Dalmatian is one of the most elegant and aristocratic dogs. Through proper breeding he has become a very graceful animal, with much strength and agility in all his movements. There is nothing more pleasing to the eye than to see a Dalmatian running free, with beauty, swiftness, and strength.

His activities and names have been as varied as his supposed origins. He has been a guard dog, a coach dog, a shepherd, a firehouse mascot, and a house pet. He has also been used as a hunting dog, a draft dog, a circus clown and a performer. His willingness to please is what has led him to his various occupations. Some of his nicknames include Plum Pudding Dog, Firehouse Dog, Coach Dog, Carriage Dog, and the Spotted Dick, to name only a few.

No matter what name or origin is applied to the beautiful spotted dog, he is still the one and only true Coach Dog that we know of:

Important Facts in the Dalmatian Timeline

1780 First printed word *Dalmatian* in the English language.

1787 George Washington purchases a Coach Dog stud for his wife's Dalmatian bitch.

Adopted as the mascot of fire companies around the U.S., the Dalmatian has served man with loyalty and dedication.

Oil painting of four champions from Lyco Dalmatians.

1790 First British writer to use the word *Dalmatian*, Thomas Bewick in *A General History of Quadrupeds.*

1860 Dog show classes first held for Dalmatians in England on December 3rd and 4th.

1888 First Dalmatian registered with the American Kennel Club.

1890 First British Dalmatian club formed.

1890 First official standard published in England.

1904 Dalmatian Club of America formed with 26 members.

1905 Dalmatian Club of America elected as a member of the AKC.

1956 Dodie Smith's *The Hundred and One Dalmatians* published.

1961 Walt Disney's animated cartoon *101 Dalmatians* released.

1968 Ch. Fanhill Faune owned by Mrs. E. J. Woodyatt became Supreme Champion at Crufts.

Firsts in Dalmatian History

First Dalmatian registered with the AKC was Bessie owned by Mrs. N.L. Havey.

First Dalmatian registered as a result of completing his championship was Ch. Hoyt owned by J.M. Schontz.

First Dalmatian champion confirmed by the AKC was Ch. Edgecomb D' Artagnan, a male, owned by M.W. Martin.

Dalmatians have achieved much for their breed. This Dal easily clears a jump with a dumbbell in his mouth in obedience.

The first bitch to become a champion was Spotted Diamond owned by M.W. Martin. First imported Dalmatian champion was Ch. Windy Valley Snowstorm owned by Windy Valley Kennels, N.Y.

First Non-Sporting Group winner was Tally-Ho Last of Sunstar.

First DCA National Specialty was won by Ch. Tally-Ho Last of Sunstar.

First Dalmatian entered in obedience classes was Captain Fiske owned by Louis Geddes Fiske.

First Dalmatian to achieve a Companion Dog degree was Meeker's Barbara Worth owned by G.S. Walker.

First Dalmatian to earn a Companion Dog Excellent and Utility Dog was Io owned by H. and L. Meistrell.

First Dalmatian champion to earn a Companion Dog title was Ch. Byron's Penny owned by Robert Byron.

CHARACTERISTICS of the Dalmatian

The role of the Dalmatian in today's society has changed greatly since his use as a coach dog. Since we no longer ride in carriages pulled by horses, nor do firehouses have horse-drawn trucks, the Dalmatian has lost his true occupation. He is not a hunting dog or a guard dog, and he is only used occasionally for therapy or rescue work. His main role in today's society is as a family companion and friend, a job he does extremely well and takes very seriously.

He is a medium-sized, smooth-coated dog, a hardy breed whose day-to-day care is neither involved nor fussy. The Dalmatian comes in two acceptable coat colors: black and white and liver and white; the black spotting being the dominant color in the breed. Both colors are acceptable for showing and breeding purposes, and there is no difference in disposition between the colors. It is only a matter of personal preference as to which color Dalmatian you purchase.

Of all the dogs I have owned and shown in my life, none is as loyal or as loving as the Dalmatian. They are dogs with undying love for their owners, young and old

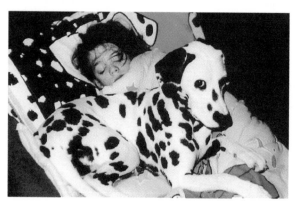

The Dalmatian is a dog with undying love for its owner. This is Lyco's Dream Girl looking over a small member of the family.

alike. They seem to be aware of each person's weaknesses and strengths. I've seen a very active young Dal be as gentle as a kitten with an elderly person or young child, walking slowly so as not to hurt or knock over, kissing little faces and old wrinkled hands. Then again, I've seen them be happy and bouncy, playing ball or fetch with a group of young

This Dal is not quite sure what his feline friend has in mind.

people. Their energy and love know no bounds. Dalmatians seem to have an uncanny way of knowing how to treat each individual.

The Dalmatian is very in tune to human emotions. If you are happy and carefree, he will join along with you in your enthusiasm and energy. One amazing characteristic is the Dalmatian "smile," showing a full set of teeth when he is happy. There is nothing like coming home from a long day to be greeted by a smiling Dal.

When you are tired and need to rest, he will be by your feet or, better yet, on your lap if allowed. A Dalmatian needs to be touching his owner. You can be standing doing dishes and he will be leaning against your legs. He loves affection. If your mood is one of sadness, he will display the same feelings and his eyes will reflect your unhappiness. I have one Dal who when he sees me crying will not allow any of the other dogs to come near me, not even enter the same room.

When your are sick, his greatest joy will be to lie next to you in bed, and try to help share your discomfort. He is indeed a loving animal. As I tell all future puppy buyers, a Dal needs to be close to his owners as much as possible. He does not care what you are busy doing, he must be part of the activity.

This is most definitely a "people dog." This is not a

breed to be left outside away from the family. He needs to be considered a part of the family, preferably the center of attention whenever possible. If left alone outside, chained to a tree, or ignored, he will pine away. If your idea of owning a dog is a pat on the head once a day and feeding the animal, this is not the breed for you.

Dalmatians adjust to all sorts of lifestyles. Whether you live in the country or in the city, they will be happy as long as they have time with their owners. Although Dals love and need exercise, if you are a city dweller a good long walk and a run in the park on a daily basis will help your dog be healthy and happy. If you live in a suburban area with a large backyard, I do recommend fencing in an area so your dog can be allowed to have free run and exercise and still be safe. Country living is an ideal situation for any dog. It is a pleasure to drive through a country setting and see a Dalmatian running with a horse, a throwback from yesteryear. It's always amazing me to take a Dal to a horse farm, introduce him to the horses for the first time, and see how naturally he reacts. The Coach Dog is alive and well and living inside every Dalmatian!

An unfenced area is a potential danger to your Dal. Be sure to keep a close eye on your Dalmatian when running in open areas.

Your Dalmatian also enjoys all sorts of weather. He will love to swim in a lake or pool and will be just as pleased with a romp and tumble in the snow. They are, however, not equipped to be left outside during the cold months for any length of time. Their coat is not thick or heavy enough to protect them from freezing weather conditions. One must use common sense in outside activities, both in extreme cold and heat.

Dalmatians are moderately active dogs and tend to wander if left unattended. Therefore never leave your Dal unattended in a situation where he can explore on his own, for he can quickly become lost.

Again, anyone can be an ideal owner for the wonderful spotted dog. Your main prerequisite is to be willing to give quality time and love to your new friend.

Even in the depths of winter a Dalmatian needs plenty of time to exercise. This is Lyco's Buster waiting for the spring thaw.

People often ask, "What if we work all day?" In today's society, with everyone working, no one would own a dog. My response is always to give plenty of quality time and attention and you will have a very happy and healthy dog.

The Dalmatian was once used as a guard dog. Today, as your family pet, you will find him to be an excellent watchdog. He will be tentative toward newcomers to your home until he realizes and is reassured that they are friends.

Dalmatians are not a typical "barky dog." If your Dal

is making noise, there is always a reason and you should check it out and investigate what is troubling him.

The only work the Dalmatian of today performs is that of being a show dog, a job he does extremely well and seems to enjoy tremendously. The Dalmatian is a "showy dog," and showing-off in the ring seems to suit him just fine. Whether it is in the breed ring or obedience ring, Dals love to show-off, just as they did as performers for the gypsies and minstrels. I do believe they enjoy the sport of showing because of the close interaction between human and dog.

The Dalmatian is generally easy to train. Praise him lavishly whenever he does something right.

The Dalmatian is generally happy and friendly with a gentleness about him, which makes him easy to train. A harsh tone of voice is usually all that is needed to correct him, which will

cause him to give you the "hang dog" look of apology.

Dalmatians tend to bond more closely with one member of the family, but are not considered a one-man dog. They are suited to all types of households and are generally friendly to everyone. They are not aggressive by nature, but in the right situation they will be great protectors.

The basic character of the Dalmatian is friendly and fun-loving. He is an extrovert (except to total strangers) who is anxious to please, extremely affectionate, and intelligent—a dog who can be controlled by patience, love and kindness.

QUESTIONS FREQUENTLY ASKED ABOUT THE DALMATIAN

Q. What is the difference between liver-spotted dogs and black-spotted dogs?

A. There is no difference. It is only a matter of color preference to the individual who is purchasing the dog. The only unacceptable color is the tri-colored dog, which has both liver and black spots, and he can neither be shown nor bred. The black spotting is the dominant gene color.

Q. How long does a Dalmatian live?

A. The average life expectancy is between 12 and 15 years, but it is not unusual for a Dal to live late in his teens—17 to 18.

Q. How large is a Dalmatian?

A. Males tend to be larger, with an average height of 23 to 24 inches at the shoulder, and weigh between 50 to 60 pounds. Females are smaller, anywhere from 19 to 23 inches, weighing between 40 to 50 pounds.

Q. Do Dalmatians like children?

A. Yes. Most dogs like children, unless teased or abused by a child. All children must be taught to treat a puppy or adult dog with respect and love. A Dal will protect a child with great care.

Q. Are all Dalmatians deaf?

A. Absolutely NOT ! This is a congenital defect that

occurs at a minimal rate. Breeders will be able to tell at an early age which puppy is deaf. Today, most reputable breeders have all litters hearing-tested.

Q. Are all Dalmatians hyper?

A. No. They are an active and happy breed that likes and needs exercise. With the proper training and daily exercise, you will have a very well-behaved dog.

Q. Do they shed?

A Dalmatian's first and ultimate goal in life is to please his owner. This Dal will do anything for his biscuit!

With the proper training and daily exercise, a Dal can be a very well-behaved dog off-lead.

A. Yes, they shed lightly all year 'round. With regular brushing and a little care your dog will be extremely clean.

Q. How much will my Dal eat?

A. Puppies require three small

Dalmatian puppies eat three times a day, while an adult will be satisfied with two smaller meals.

meals a day, until six months of age. An adult dog only requires two equal meals per day, one in the morning and one at night.

Q. Do Dalmatians like to travel?

A. Yes, Dals love to accompany their owners everywhere they go. After the initial puppy carsickness, you will have a great travel companion.

Q. Do they require expensive medical care?

A. No, usually a routine (once a year) checkup is all that is required. This will include yearly booster shots, worm check, and blood work for heartworm.

TRIBUTE TO A DALMATIAN

This Last Will and Testament was written by Eugene O'Neill in memory and honor of his beloved Dalmatian,

Blemie. Eugene O'Neill was a four-time Pulitzer Prize winner. He wrote more than thirty plays. The Last Will and Testament of Silverdene Emblem O'Neill was first printed in 1956, and reprinted in 1959 by the Yale University Press.

I, Silverdene Emblem O'Neill (familiarly known to my family and friends and acquaintances as Blemie), because the burden of my years and infirmities is heavy upon me, and I realize the end of my life is near, do hearby bury my last will and testament in the mind of my Master. He will not know it is there until after I am dead. Then, remembering me in his loneliness, he will suddenly know of this testament, and I

The loyalty of a Dalmatian to its owner cannot be overstated. One look into your canine friend's eyes will show a lifetime of trust and friendship.

ask him then to inscribe it as a memorial to me.

I have little in the way of material things to leave. Dogs are wiser than men. They do not set great store upon things. They do not waste their days hoarding property. They do not ruin their sleep worrying about how to keep the objects they have, and to obtain the objects they have not. There is nothing of value I have to bequeath except my love and my faith. This I leave to all those who have loved me, to my Master and Mistress, who I know will mourn me most, to Freeman who has been so good to me, to Cyn and Roy and Willie and Naomi and—but if I should list all those who have loved me it would force my Master to write a book. Perhaps it is vain of me to boast when I am so near death, which returns all beasts and vanities to dust, but I have always been an extremely lovable dog.

I ask my Master and Mistress to remember me always, but not to grieve for me too long. In my life I have tried to be a comfort to them in time of sorrow, and a reason for added joy in their happiness. It is painful for me to think that even in death I should cause them pain. Let them remember that while no dog has ever had a happier life (and this I owe to their love and care for me), now that I have grown blind and deaf and lame, and even my sense of smell fails me so that a rabbit could be right under my nose and I might not know, my pride has sunk to a sick, bewildered humiliation. I feel life is taunting me with having over-lingered my welcome. It is time I said good-bye, before I become too sick a burden on myself and on those who love me. It will be sorrow to leave them, but not sorrow to die. Dogs do not fear death as men do. We accept it as a part of life, not as something alien and terrible which destroys life. What may come after death, who knows? I would like to believe with those of my fellow Dalmatians who are devout Mohammedans, that there is a Paradise where one is always young and full-bladdered; where all the day one dillies and dallies with an amorous multitude of houris, beautifully spotted; where jack rabbits that run fast but not too fast (like the houris) are as the sands of the desert; where each blissful hour is

Dalmatians of all ages are fun-loving and playful. These three pups are having a great time romping through their yard.

mealtime; where in long evenings there are a million fireplaces with logs forever burning, and one curls oneself up and blinks into the flames and nods and dreams, remembering the old brave days on earth, and the love of one's Master and Mistress.

I am afraid this is too much for even such a dog as I am to expect. But peace, at least, is certain. Peace and long rest for weary old heart and head

Next to spending quality time with his owner, the Dalmatian loves to dream. This is Lyco's Princess Daisy caught taking a short snooze.

and limbs, and eternal sleep in the earth I have loved so well. Perhaps, after all, this is best.

One last request I earnestly make. I have heard my Mistress say, " When Blemie dies we must never have another dog. I love him so much I could never love another one." Now I would ask her, for love of me, to have another. It would be a poor tribute to my memory never to have a dog again. What I would like to feel is that, having once had me in the family, now she cannot live without a dog! I have never had a narrow jealous spirit. I have always held that most dogs are good (and one cat, the black one I have permitted to share the living room rug during the evenings, whose affection I have tolerated in a kindly spirit, and in rare sentimental moods, even reciprocated a trifle). Some dogs, of course, are better than others. Dalmatians, naturally, as everyone knows, are best. So I suggest a Dalmatian as my successor. He can hardly be as well bred or as well mannered or as distinguished and handsome as I was in my prime. My Master and Mistress would not ask the impossible. But he will do his best, I am sure, and even his inevitable defects will help by comparison to keep my memory green. To him I bequeath my collar and leash and my overcoat and raincoat, made to order in 1929 in Hermes in Paris. He can never wear them with the distinction I did, walking around the Place Vendome, or later along Park Avenue, all eyes fixed on me in admiration; but again I am sure he will do his utmost not to appear a mere gauche provincial dog. Here on the ranch, he might prove himself quite worthy of comparison, in some respects. He will, I presume, come closer to jack rabbits than I have been able in recent years. And, for all his faults, I hereby wish him the happiness I know will be his in my old home.

Each Dalmatian has its own individual personality. Remember to look at each dog separately for its unique characteristics.

One last word of farewell, Dear Master and Mistress. Whenever you visit my grave, say to yourselves with regret but also with happiness in your hearts at the remembrance of my long happy life with you: "Here lies one who loved us and whom we loved." No matter how deep my sleep I shall hear you, and not all the power of death can keep my spirit from wagging a grateful tail.

Tao House, December 17th, 1940.

Dalmatians of all ages know exactly how to touch their owner's hearts. This Dal, owned by the author, has much expression to his face.

STANDARD for the Dalmatian

It is only in recent days that breed standards have developed. Opinions and the appearance of breeds have changed through the centuries, and the Dalmatian's appearance has had various descriptions over the ages. These ideas also dealt with personal opinions on what was the correct standard for a breed. It was not until the founding of kennel clubs, such as the American Kennel Club, and breed clubs, that one standard was necessary and desirable.

Up until 1947, standards were concerns of various breed clubs. This caused many problems, as within a group of breed-specific clubs you could find various standards. With competition so severe between these clubs and rivalry not always very pleasant, the American Kennel Club decided to step in and create a unified standard for each breed.

A breed standard can be described as being a set criteria that defines the perfect dog of that breed. Within the standard a dog does not have to conform perfectly to be considered a dog of quality. There has never been nor likely will there ever be the *perfect dog.*

A breed standard defines certain criteria for the breed. It acts as a guide for what the "perfect" dog should look like.

The Dalmatian standard has changed many times since the early Dalmatian Club of America set its guidelines. The American Kennel Club is based upon the British standard of 1890, with varied alterations from year to year. The Kennel Club of England's standard of the Dalmatian is basically the same as the American Kennel Club's, except for two differences: Size—Dogs 23 to 24 inches, Bitches 22 to 23 inches; Fault—Blue eyes.

The Kennel Club of England and the American Kennel Club only differ in their standard of the Dalmatian regarding size and eye colors permissible (the UK faults blue eyes).

In the booklet titled *Dalmatians* by Mr. H. Fred Lauer, in 1907, he speaks about color in the Dalmatian and the number of black ears at birth. He expounds on the correlation between black ears and poorly spotted dogs, and the correlation between well spotted ears and poorly marked dogs. He had no objection to black ears, a far cry from the standard of today. In the early stages of development of the standard in the United States, spotting was not considered very important; show dogs of yesteryear would be sold as pet puppies today. Markings make up 25 percent of today's standard.

AMERICAN KENNEL CLUB STANDARD

General Appearance

The Dalmatian is a distinctively spotted dog; poised and alert; strong, muscular and active; free of shyness; intelligent in expression; symmetrical in outline; without exaggeration or coarseness. The Dalmatian is capable of great endurance, combined with a great amount of speed. Deviations from the described ideal

should be penalized in direct proportion to the degree of deviation.

Size, Proportion, Substance

Desirable height at the withers is between 19 and 23 inches. Undersize or oversize is a fault. Any dog or bitch over 24 inches at the withers is disqualified. The overall length of the body from the forechest to the buttocks is approximately equal to the height of the withers. The Dalmatian has a good substance and is strong and sturdy in bone, but never coarse.

Head

The head is in balance with the overall dog. It is of fair length and is free of loose skin. The Dalmatian's *expression* is alert and intelligent, indicating a stable

Dalmatian puppies are miniature versions of their parents. Prior to bringing home your new charge ask the breeder of your Dal's lineage.

and outgoing temperament. The *eyes* are set moderately well apart, are medium sized and somewhat rounded in appearance, and are set well into the skull. Eye color is brown, or blue, or any combination thereof; the darker the better and usually darker in black-spotted than in liver-spotted dogs. Abnormal position of the eyelids or eyelashes (ectropion, entropion, trichiasis) is a major fault. Incomplete pigmentation around the eye rims is a major fault.

The *ears* are of moderate size, proportionately wide at the base and gradually tapering to a rounded tip. They are set rather high, and are carried close to the head, and are thin and fine in texture. When the Dalmatian is alert, the top of the ear is level with the top of the skull and the tip of the ear reaches to the bottom of the line of the cheek. The top of

Alert ears of the Dalmatian are level with the top of the skull, and the tip of the ear will reach to the bottom line of the cheek.

the skull is flat with a slight vertical furrow and is approximately as wide as it is long. The **stop** is moderately well defined. The cheeks blend smoothly into a powerful muzzle, the top of which is level and parallel to the top of the skull. The **muzzle** and top of the skull are about equal length. The **nose** is completely pigmented on the leather, black in black-spotted dogs, and brown in liver-spotted dogs. Incomplete nose pigmentation is a major fault. The **lips** are clean and close fitting. The teeth meet in a **scissors bite**. Overshot bites are disqualifications.

Neck, Topline, Body

The Dalmatian is a very alert and graceful-looking animal with a long neck which tapers into a deep chest.

The **neck** is nicely arched, fairly long, free from throatiness, and blends smoothly into the shoulders. The **topline** is smooth. The **chest** is deep, capacious, and of moderate width, having good spring of rib without being barrel shaped. The brisket reaches to the elbow. The underline of the rib cage curves gradually to a moderate tuck-up. The **back** is level and strong. The **loin** is short, muscular and slightly arched. The flanks narrow through the loin. The **croup** is nearly level with the back. The **tail** is a natural expression of the topline. It is not inserted too low down. It is strong at the insertion and tapers to the tip, which reaches to the hock. It is never docked. The tail is carried with a slight upward curve but should never curl over the back. Ring tails and low-set tails are faults.

Forequarters

The **shoulders** are smoothly muscled and well laid back. The **upper arm** is approximately equal in length to the shoulder blade and joins it at an angle sufficient to insure that the foot falls under the shoulder. The **elbows** are close to the body. The **legs** are straight, strong and sturdy in bone. There is a slight angle at the **pastern** denoting flexibility.

The Dalmatian looks powerful and muscular at every angle he is viewed.

Hindquarters

The **hindquarters** are powerful, having smooth, yet well defined muscles. The **stifle** is well bent. The **hocks** are well let down. When the Dalmatian is standing, the hind legs, viewed from the rear, are parallel to each other from the point of the hock to the heel of the pad. Cowhocks are a major fault.

Feet

Feet are very important. Both front and rear feet are round and compact with thick, elastic pads, and well arched toes. Flat feet are a major fault. Toenails are black and or white in black-spotted dogs, and brown and or white in liver-spotted dogs. Dewclaws may be removed.

Coat

The **coat** is short, dense, fine and close fitting, it is neither woolly nor silky, it is sleek, glossy and healthy in appearance.

Color and Markings

Color and markings and their overall appearance are very important points to be evaluated. The ground color is pure white. In black-spotted dogs the spots are black, in liver-spotted dogs the spots are liver brown. Any color markings other than black or liver are disqualified. **Spots** are round and well defined, the more distinct the better. They vary from the size of a dime to the size of a half dollar. They are pleasingly and evenly distributed. The less the spots intermingle the better. Spots are usually smaller on the head, legs, and tail then on the body. Ears are preferably spotted. **Tri-color** (which occurs rarely in the breed) is a disqualification. It consists of tan markings found on the head, neck, chest, leg or tail of black or liver-spotted dogs. Bronzing of black spots, fading and or darkening of the liver spots due to environmental conditions or normal process of coat change are not tri-colorization. **Patches** are a disqualification. A patch is a solid mass of black or

Black or liver-colored spots are the only permissible colors according to the standard for the breed. This quartet beautifully exhibits both colors.

liver hair containing no white hair. It is appreciably larger than a normal size spot. Patches are a dense, brilliant color with sharply defined, smooth edges. Patches are present at birth. Large masses formed by intermingled or overlapping spots are not patches. Such masses should indicate individual spots by uneven edges and/or white hairs scattered throughout the mass.

Gait

In keeping with the Dalmatian's historical use as a coach dog, gait and endurance are of great importance. Movement is steady and effortless. Balanced angulation fore and aft combined with powerful muscles and good condition produce smooth, efficient action. There is a powerful drive from the rear coordinated with extended reach in the front. The topline remains level. Elbows, hocks, and feet turn neither in nor out. As the speed of the trot increases, there is a tendency to single track.

Temperament

Temperament is stable and outgoing, yet dignified. Shyness is a major fault.

Balanced angulation combined with powerful muscles and good condition produce smooth efficient action in the Dalmatian.

Scale of Points

General appearance	5
Size, proportion, substance	10
Head	10
Neck, topline, body	10
Forequarters	5
Hindquarters	5
Feet	5
Coat	5
Color and markings	25
Gait	10
Temperament	10
TOTAL	100

Be sure to reward your Dal for a job well done. Rewards will reinforce training and enhance the learning process.

Your Dalmatian puppy can be a champion of the future, so train him well and reward him properly.

Disqualifications

Any dog or bitch over 24 inches at the withers.

Overshot or undershot bites.

Any color markings other than black or liver.

Tri-color.

Patches.

43

SELECTING Your New Dalmatian

Before acquiring any dog, you must first research the breed you are leaning toward, and then decide whether this breed fits all your needs, and expectations. The breed you decide upon must be the correct breed for you in every respect. In the process of researching, read books on the breed, visit local breeders, and go to a dog show and talk with the owners and handlers of that specific breed. Be sure you are absolutely certain about the breed in question, as this decision will affect you and your dog for many years to come.

Dalmatians are smooth-coated, medium-sized dogs with a gentle temperament and a great deal of devotion for their owners.

The Dalmatian is a short-haired, smooth-coated, medium-sized dog. He is an ideal family pet—a dog who is intelligent and devoted to his owner. He is also moderately territorial. The Dalmatian is a clean animal, but he does shed moderately all year 'round. He is also a fun-loving and active dog who loves nothing better than a good run in the park or yard.

When choosing your Dalmatian, you must decide whether you want a show dog or a pet. Showing is very rewarding. It is a lot of fun for the entire family, but it is very time consuming and takes a lot of dedication. Whether you decide on a pet dog or one with show potential, you will want to purchase the best dog you can. Even the pet-dog owner wants not only a dog that he can be proud of, but one that is healthy and a good representative of the breed. Another important factor in choosing a good specimen of the breed is that it begins the education of the new owner with this specific breed. If one acquires a bad specimen, it will leave an everlasting bad impression. On the other hand, a good

Have your new Dalmatian thoroughly checked for all health problems prior to bringing it home. An ounce of prevention is worth a pound of cure.

animal will create a favorable reaction to the chosen breed.

As with any breed of dog, there are a few things that you should be aware of in regard to health problems in the Dalmatian. One is congenital deafness. This occurs at a minimal rate and today most reputable breeders have their litters' hearing-tested at various medical facilities around the country. When purchasing your Dal, ask for a copy of his hearing test if the breeder has had the litter tested. If not, be sure to mention that you are aware of the deafness in Dalmatians and want to know what kind of testing has been performed on the litter. If a deaf puppy is found, he must never be sold. Do not get a deaf dog, even if it is given to you. It is a lot of work and specialized training is required to rear the dog properly– you are only setting yourself up for a big heartache.

More and more research is being done on the hearing problems in Dalmatians and hopefully someday it will be eliminated from the breed. Some Dals are what is called unilateral, which means they hear from only one ear. Again, this occurs at a minimal rate and the breeder will be able to tell you if the pup is a "uni." The unilateral Dal lives a perfectly normal life, and at a very early age he will adjust so well that you will never know he has a hearing defect. The unilateral dog makes a fine and healthy pet but should never be bred.

Hearing problems are being researched in Dalmatians and hopefully will one day be eliminated from the breed. Be sure that any puppy you purchase has had its hearing tested.

The other peculiarity in the Dalmatian is the direct excretion of uric acid by the kidneys without the conversion into water soluble urea. This is due to the metabolic difference in this breed. The only consequence of this irregularity is that a small percentage of males may develop kidney or bladder stones. This condition almost never occurs in females. Various corrective diets and medications have now been developed to combat this condition, giving dogs with this problem a normal life span and a healthy life. This, like the deafness, occurs at a minimal rate, some lines carrying it more than others.

Some research finds a significant link between feeding high-protein diets and the formation of stones. It is always recommended that your Dalmatian be kept on a good-quality kibble that is low in protein.

Occasionally, some Dalmatians will experience skin and coat problems during the summer months. Redness, scratching and loss of hair can usually be traced to a specific source. These skin problems tend to be inherited, so when purchasing a puppy, get a good look at the parents if at all possible.

Other than the above-mentioned peculiarities, Dalmatians do not have any serious problems that are found in other breeds, such as hip dysplasia, eye problems, etc. They are usually good eaters and do not require expensive supplements to keep them healthy. Dalmatians have a good life expectancy, as high as 15 years.

A litter of Dalmatian puppies makes it difficult to choose just one. Be very careful in your selection and if possible always view the parents.

PUPPY OR ADULT

If you have done all your research, and have decided the Dalmatian is the breed for you, your next important decision is whether to get a puppy or an adult dog. There are both positive and negative problems when acquiring an adult or a puppy, and you must be the one to decide which is the best for your personal situation and how much time and energy you are willing to give your new pet.

To decide on either a puppy or an adult, a prospective owner should assess his personal situation and see which one he is more suited for.

Let's begin with the puppy. A puppy is a four-legged baby and needs a great deal of time and attention. They must be housebroken, meaning taught what is acceptable behavior and what is not. As I tell all puppy buyers, puppies poop, chew, scratch and cause all sorts of mischief for at least seven months to a year—so be prepared! However, by obtaining a puppy rather than an adult you are the one who will be training him to your standards. It will be you who is the one molding his temperament. Watching your puppy develop into a fine, obedient, and loving pet will give you great satisfaction. He will grow to be devoted to you and your family.

You must also realize that a puppy will need much more time and energy in raising, more trips outside, and more meals to be fed. Your mornings will begin much earlier than usual. The joy of watching your puppy grow into a fine, aristocratic dog will be a lifetime memory and a great reward for all your time and patience.

By all means, please do not rush out to buy a puppy without thoroughly thinking it through. If you have definitely decided on a puppy, visit as many litters as possible. Look very carefully at the litter as a whole. Are the puppies kept clean? Are they in a safe and well-ventilated area preferably around people (not isolated in a barn or a cellar away from all human contact)? This aspect of a puppy's initial care will be very important in his later interaction with people. Check the reaction of

Once you have decided a Dalmatian is the breed for you, visit as many litters as possible so you can make an educated choice.

the puppies to your approach. They should not shy away but rather run to greet you. This will be a good indication whether their first few weeks of life with human contact have been favorable.

If at all possible, you should observe the dam, even if it is from a distance. Many new mothers will not allow strangers to get too near their puppies. Check what condition she is in. Is she clean, well nourished and happy? A sickly bitch can also mean sickly puppies. All these criteria will help you in choosing a healthy puppy.

Early socialization is very important in a puppy's development. In any puppy you are considering, check his reaction to your approach; tons of kisses are a good sign.

If you are planning to purchase a show-quality puppy, you must expect to pay more. The breeder may require you to breed the dog if it turns out to be of high quality. Remember that your show dog will also be your family pet.

In the Dalmatian breed, there is something called a "patch," which is a puppy or dog with a very large black area usually around the head, mainly over the ear or the eye or both. The texture of the fur in this area will also be different, much more dense. This is a major fault in the breed and these dogs can never be bred or shown. They do make wonderful pets and have no unusual health problems other than the usual Dalmatian peculiarities.

The following are several important health points to check when choosing a puppy:

1. The puppy should be well fed, filled out, solid, not pot-bellied, and certainly not skinny.

2. The puppy's eyes should be clear and bright. Check them for redness or discharge. This could

indicate an infection or that one is about to occur.

Some owners choose to adopt an adult instead of a puppy. Adults require patience and consistencey.

3. The pup's nose should be moist and free of discharge.

4. Check the teeth. They should be free from stains and discoloration, as well as any obvious irregularities. A puppy up to five months has milk teeth. After they fall out, he will have his permanent teeth. Teeth should be white and gums should be a healthy pink.

5. Be careful of a pup that is listless and has dull eyes—he may be full of parasites.

6. Check the inside of the ears. They should be clean, without dirt or any redness or irritation.

7. The skin and coat are good indications of health. The coat should be shiny and skin clear and free of parasites. Check for fleas and ticks. Blotches on the skin may indicate poor health.

8. Shyness is not a good sign. It may indicate rough

handling or lack of socialization.

9. Look also for any deformation in joints and also check for crooked legs.

10. If viewing a litter, be sure to observe any stool present. Diarrhea can be an indication of an unhealthy litter or puppy.

Judging a healthy adult dog will be very similar as judging a puppy. The main difference to be noted is his temperament. Be sure he is friendly. Acting a little tentative is fine, but a very aggressive or shy dog can lead to problems later on.

An adult dog is usually set in his ways and has learned his basic rules and standards of living from whomever raised him from a pup. It will take an older dog a longer time to adjust to a new home situation than it will a puppy.

The puppy you pick should be well fed with clear eyes, moist nose, and clean ears and coat.

When going to view the prospective adult Dalmatian,

approach him slowly. You are a stranger, and he is likely to be a bit cautious, but given time most dogs will warm up to you very quickly. Any adult you acquire will come with his or her own personality traits learned from the previous owner. Be willing to take a little more time with the adult in some areas of training.

Most adult dogs are housebroken and are past the destructive age, although the transition into a new home situation can sometimes cause a little regression in behavior. An adult dog is usually satisfied with being left alone more than a puppy is. Take all these things into consideration before acquiring an adult.

If you have decided upon an adult, there are several questions you should ask yourself. Why is someone selling or giving away this dog? Is he a biter? Is he uncontrollable? Is the bitch pregnant? Does he have any serious illnesses that will require medical attention? An adult dog can certainly give a great deal of joy but be careful of where he is coming from. Some breeders place older dogs that are wonderful animals only because their kennel or breeding programs can only handle so many animals. There are also organizations that have rescue shelters from where someone can acquire a wonderful adult due to someone's moving or a death in the family.

Even when you purchase an adult Dalmatian, you should receive a health certificate for the animal.

Whether purchasing a puppy or an adult dog, you should be given a health certificate on the animal. This should include information on vaccination dates, when and what was used in worming, and when the next shots are due. A three-generation pedigree and a bill of sale should also be included. You should also be given a time limit in which you are to take the animal to your veterinarian to be checked. If he is not found to be healthy, you should have the option of returning him, with a guaranteed refund. No matter whether you get an adult or a puppy, be sure the animal is healthy and well socialized.

MALE VS. FEMALE

Before we begin with the "battle of the sexes," please disregard any and all of the old stories you have heard about male and female dogs.

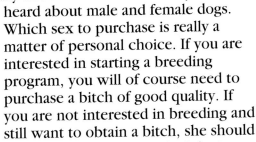

Before purchasing your Dal, be sure to consider all the differences between the two sexes and choose the one that will better complement your lifestyle.

Which sex to purchase is really a matter of personal choice. If you are interested in starting a breeding program, you will of course need to purchase a bitch of good quality. If you are not interested in breeding and still want to obtain a bitch, she should be spayed. If she is not, you must be willing to put up with her going into season twice a year.

Male dogs lift their legs to urinate on any and all of your shrubs and flowers. If you are an avid gardener, this is something to consider. Also, a whole male, one that is not castrated, will be upset when the neighborhood bitch is in season and will roam to wherever she is if given the opportunity. Male dogs also tend to be larger, heavier, and more powerful than females.

The temperament in the Dalmatian varies from dog to dog, regardless of the sex. Sex does not enter into the aggressiveness, docility, or affection of the Dalmatian. Females are much more territorial and protective than males. Many breeders feel that males are more affectionate and that the females are more aloof. For the most part, your dog's personality traits will depend on you and how you raise him. Living with several Dalmatians of both sexes, I can tell you that each dog is an individual, just like people.

Pet puppies may come with Limited Registration which insist that they cannot be bred.

NEUTERING AND SPAYING

Neutering and spaying should be done to all dogs that are not in an active breeding program or are not actively being shown. Only quality dogs should be bred, and most reputable breeders will require you to have your pet spayed or neutered. Some breeders will keep registration papers until proof of neutering or spaying has been confirmed. This is to ensure that only dogs of the highest quality are used in the breeding program.

Spaying and neutering does not harm the animal, rather it helps retain the dog's health. Many problems can occur in unneutered animals, such as cancer and prostrate problems in males and cancer and pyometra in females.

Castration *does not* make a male less masculine. It helps to prolong his life and keeps him from roaming when a nearby bitch is in season. Many breeders feel that it also calms him down and makes him a better pet. Castration means that a male cannot produce sperm and therefore cannot reproduce. Castration does not change his physical condition.

Spaying means that a bitch cannot become pregnant or come into season. Spaying does not change her physical condition or her personality. Contrary to popular opinion, it does not make her fat or listless. Spaying also helps prevent mammary tumors and urinary-tract infections. These maladies are quite

common in unspayed females. Some unspayed bitches will also have false pregnancies after each heat cycle. All these problems can be avoided by spaying your bitch. Bitches can be spayed at any time in their lives; however, most veterinarians do feel it is better to spay a bitch at an early age.

You should not let your bitch go through a pregnancy prior to being spayed for there is less risk of mammary tumors prior to this time.

REGISTRATION AND PEDIGREES

Registration forms and pedigrees are the papers you should receive when purchasing your new puppy. Let's not get these two documents confused. Both are important in their own way. Pedigree papers, however, have nothing to do with registration forms.

Registration forms are given out by the American Kennel Club. Each breeder registers his litter, sire, dam, date of birth, number of puppies in the litter, name and address. This form is then submitted to the American Kennel Club. In return, the breeder is mailed the correct number of registration forms depending on number of puppies in the litter.

There are two types of registration forms that are supplied by the American Kennel Club to the breeder. One is called Full Registration, which states that offspring of this litter are eligible for registration in the American Kennel Club and may compete in dog shows. The other type of registration is called Limited Registration, meaning that the offspring from this litter are not eligible for registration in the American Kennel Club and entry at dog shows is restricted. The Limited Registration form is used by breeders for dogs they do not feel have the qualities to be used in breeding. This is an attempt by reputable breeders to keep only quality dogs in the breeding arena.

Be sure that you receive an American Kennel Club registration form with any purebred dog you purchase.

After receiving the registration forms, the breeder will fill each one out and give it to the new owners. The new owner will then fill out the designated areas and return the form along with the correct fee to the American Kennel Club. After several weeks, the new owner will receive a formal registration form from the American Kennel Club. The puppy is now officially on the American Kennel Club's records for purebred dogs.

Be sure when you purchase your dog, you are given an American Kennel Club registration form. This will be your proof that your dog is indeed a purebred, registered animal. It also assures you that both parents, sire and dam, are purebred dogs, as only purebreds can be registered.

A pedigree is a paper detailing your dog's ancestry. It is usually a three-generation pedigree, although you can purchase much more extensive pedigrees. A three-generation pedigree will give the novice all the information he needs. When purchasing your dog, you should always be given a three-generation pedigree. This is recommended by the American Kennel Club.

The pedigree will show you your dog's sire, dam, American Kennel Club registration number, date of birth, sex, and color. If there are any champions in his lineage, these too will be shown, enabling you to learn what is in your dog's heritage.

Pedigree papers cannot predict your dog's future, nor can they tell if he is a healthy representative of the breed, but it can give you a clear look at where he came from and the quality of the breeding that is behind him. This information will be most helpful if you are planning to show or breed your dog in the future. Knowing his heritage enables you to choose a mate that will be complementary to his line.

Puppies do not leave their dam untl eight weeks of age—it takes mom time to teach each pup the facts of life.

PUPPY TEMPERAMENT TESTING

With our preconception of what testing means—pass or fail—do not get the wrong idea of what puppy temperament testing means. This is not a test in which a puppy passes or fails. This is a test in which the reactions to various stimuli by the puppy are recorded.

Puppy temperament testing evaluates your pup's reactions to certain stimuli. The results will help breeders place their puppies into the correct homes.

The results of these tests can help the breeder select the proper home for a new puppy or even begin to decide what kind of mate will be used at breeding time. You wouldn't put a submissive, timid pup into a busy and hectic household. On the other hand, a very assertive, outgoing pup wouldn't fare well in a home with an elderly couple. The same premise holds true for breed selection. A dominant bitch will likely be paired with a more submissive stud dog and vice-versa. This test is only a guideline and can be helpful but there is no hard and fast rule that the supposed submissive puppy won't turn out to be more dominant as he matures.

Some of the stimuli used and scaled in this test, and there are variations to the test, are reactions to sound; sight sensitivity; touch sensitivity; being held up from the floor; startle response; the dominant down, which is gently holding the puppy in a down position; and people (Does he run toward you or away from you?). Each response is then evaluated and the puppy is judged on those merits. This test can be a helpful instrument in determining the puppy's basic personality.

PUPPY CARE and Training

You have now decided upon a Dalmatian puppy as your new family member. This is a big responsibility and must not be taken lightly. You must proceed with care and patience so that you may raise your puppy to become an outstanding citizen and a wonderful companion. Remember, a puppy is not a toy or a learning device but rather a loving and helpless little animal who will rely on you for the rest of his life. Be sure you go into this knowing not only that there will be much fun and happiness but that there will be equal amounts of work as well.

Your puppy needs to be placed in as many new situations as possible to be completely socialized.

Socialization means getting your puppy used to new situations, new things, and new people. His socialization should begin with the breeder and carry on to you and your family. It is the most important learning he will do.

His adjustment period begins the minute he leaves the breeder and his littermates. When you go to get him, bring along a safe carrier to take him home in. A crate is preferable, but if you do not have room in your vehicle, a box will do nicely. Holding him in your arms can only cause problems, as he will squirm and try to get loose, and this can only frighten him more. Many breeders will give you a sock or small item that has the smell of the litter on it. This will help him adjust to his new environment, as he has something familiar to associate with. Remember he is leaving everything that he has ever known. All his security is being left behind—his mother, littermates, and the breeder, his first human friend.

Upon arrival at home, let him get accustomed to the area in which he will be staying. Do not just put him in a room and disappear. Stay with him. Show him his

new bed (I do recommend using a crate), where his water bowl is, and the area in which he is to relieve himself. Make sure to have a few safe toys and chew devices scattered around, such as Nylabone® and Gumabone® Pooch Pacifiers®.

Be sure you receive from the seller a daily schedule, including when he eats, how much he eats, and most importantly *what* he eats. Do not change food, as this will upset his entire system. Always use the food the seller recommends.

Slowly acquaint him with the area he is to use as the bathroom. Be sure to always use the same area. This will help him to know that this area is solely for the use of relieving himself, which will be a great help in housebreaking the puppy. His play area outside should not be the same as his bathroom area. He will very quickly make the distinction if you are consistent in your routine of training.

The first night is usually the most difficult for your new arrival. He may whimper only for a short period of time or all night. The main thing you can give him at this point is patience and love. Give him his own bed. If you have purchased a crate, leave the door open so he has the freedom to go in and out. Keep him, of course, in a safely confined area, such as a washroom or kitchen, that is gated from the rest of the house. No puppy should have free run of the house until he is

The first night you bring your new puppy home will be most difficult. Give him plenty of patience and love, and his own bed too.

completely trained. When he begins to whimper, try not to go to him at first. Most puppies quiet down after a short period of time. I do not recommend taking him in bed with you as this will set guidelines for the future, and may cause unnecessary problems. Remember, bad habits are very difficult to break later on down the line.

Your new puppy should not be permitted to sleep in your bed unless you wish him to do so as an adult.

Always use his name when calling him. A short name followed by the command of "come" is easiest for the puppy. He will very quickly associate the name with the word "come." Do not use a long sentence when calling your puppy, it will only confuse him; short, one-word commands are the best.

Introduce the collar at an early age. It will need to be adjusted regularly as the puppy grows.

Next step is the collar. Be sure you purchase a very soft puppy collar. Place it around his neck—not too tightly, as you will choke him; not too loose, as he will get caught in it. *Always use your Dalmatian puppy's name when teaching him to "come."*
A usual rule of thumb is to allow enough room for two fingers. In the beginning he will scratch at the collar and try to bite it. Divert his attention by giving him a toy or just by playing with him. In a day or two he will not even notice that he is wearing a collar.

Leash training is a little more involved. I do not recommend that you put a leash on him the first day, unless you must do so to exercise him. When you begin leash training, proceed very slowly. Do not yank or pull the pup. Gently give little tugs or coax him to walk next to you by using a toy or playful gesture. Always walk the puppy on your left side. A puppy who has had an initial bad experience will not be a happy animal on a leash. First impressions often can be lasting ones. With slow and patient training, within a few days to a week you will have a dog who will look forward to his walks on the leash.

After the puppy has had all his basic shots, the most important part of training will begin. You must begin exposing him to all sorts of situations. Take him out with you whenever possible, let people pet him and fuss over him, take him in the car for rides, take him to shopping centers and parks, and expose him to as many different situations as possible. You want your puppy to learn that people and things are not frightening but rather enjoyable and pleasurable. A dog who is always left alone or only with his owners will become shy and timid and occasionally aggressive. He must learn to trust people and new situations. Of course when doing these things, do so with extreme care and caution and do not force the puppy.

The best way to teach your Dal puppy not to be frightened of new experiences is to introduce him to new environments (and interesting people).

The most important thing in socializing and training your puppy is love and patience. This is a four-legged baby who has no idea what is expected of him, nor does he know what is right or wrong. He is not destructive because he is mean or trying to get even but only because he has not been trained to know what you want and what is acceptable behavior. It is your job to train him properly.

HOUSEBREAKING

Training a puppy at anything is a slow and gradual process, and housebreaking requires the ultimate in patience. No puppy is born housebroken, and no puppy becomes housebroken without a lot of work, time, and patience. Dalmatians tend to be very clean dogs and are usually very easy to housebreak, if it is done properly. When you begin, take the puppy out at regular intervals: after eating, after he wakes up from sleeping, after he has eaten, and when you see him going around

Crate-training is the easiest form of housebreaking. Many breeders insist that new owners purchase a crate and train their puppies accordingly.

in circles. Always take the puppy to the same area outside every time, wait for him to relieve himself, and then make a big fuss over him. Do not play with him while you are waiting for him to go—play with him *after* he has gone. He must realize that he is in this area for one reason and one reason alone. After he has gone, then you can play with him, but not in the same area that you are using for his toilet. If the puppy has an accident in the house, and he will, just take him to the accident area and say, "no," then bring him

Your puppy should be taken outside to eliminate. Be sure to give him extra praise when he does this.

Do not fuss or play with your Dalmatian puppy while you are waiting for him to eliminate. Ignore him until he has gone, and play with him after.

back outside to his "special area."

Paper training can be a very useful tool, especially if you are away from the house for extended periods of time, such as when you are at work. Always place the paper in the same area every time. The puppy must have an area to relive himself when no one is around to take him out. Little by little, as he gains bladder and bowel control, you will have a housebroken puppy. Most dogs are not totally housebroken before six to nine months of age. Be sure your puppy has fresh water at all times during the day, but remove water at bedtime and after he goes out for the last time in the evening.

Every puppy should learn to spend time in a crate. This should be a slow process. After the puppy has played and is tired, place him in the crate. He will usually go to sleep. As soon as he awakens, he will cry, and this is your clue to take him outside to his "special area"— immediately. You can increase crate time as the puppy becomes accustomed to it, and is closer to being housebroken. Most puppies and dogs alike will learn to love their crates and will go in on their own accord. Remember, dogs are den animals. The crate becomes his den, a place to retreat to. Never use the crate as a punishment. It is used as a training device, which, when used properly, will become the dog's home. Most adult dogs who have been raised with crates can be crated for hours and also overnight.

A puppy will soon learn to love his house or crate and will retreat to it on his own for naps and refuge from the family.

Repetition and consistency are your key factors in training. Say what you mean and say it clearly and firmly. Dogs do not need a lengthy sentence and will not benefit from that or your impatience. Remember, what you put into your dog, you will get out! A well-trained dog will be your greatest reward.

There are several things to remember when training a puppy. A puppy is not a toy that is to be cared for and played with and then neglected and pushed aside. A puppy is not a novelty—he is your responsibility. A puppy does not clean himself—he needs constant care. A puppy is not a device for a child to learn responsibility— he is a living creature with many needs. Most of all, a puppy is only little for a very short time, so enjoy him for who he is and for who he is going to become.

GROWTH OF A PUPPY

A puppy grows at a very rapid pace, with each stage overlapping the previous one. In one year a puppy develops at a pace almost equivalent to a seven-year-old child. Your attention to a young puppy will focus around several major areas: feeding, inoculations, housebreaking and early training.

The most notable change in a puppy will be his awake and sleep periods. When you first bring a young puppy home, he will sleep much more of the time *Dalmatian puppies are among the most active and curious of all puppies.* than he will play. This is perfectly normal. Most puppies leave their litters at around seven weeks of age, so they are still very newly developed creatures. Your new puppy will tire easily, and a short play period will tire him out for hours. As he grows he will sleep less and play more.

The puppy's development is moving rapidly. At around three to five months he will begin to lose his milk teeth (baby teeth) and will acquire his permanent teeth. At this time he will be chewing and biting constantly, due to the discomfort on his gums. Be sure to give him a safe chew toy to try to keep him busy. Gumabones® are usually best for puppies due to their softer composition. These baby teeth feel like sharp little razors when he begins to

chew on you. This is not an act of aggression, only an attempt to ease his discomfort. Tell him

Gumabones® are great safe toys for puppies. They satisfy the need to chew and are of a soft composition so as not to harm their tender gums.

"no" and give him a chew toy.

By the time he is around four months old, he will begin to take on his own personality and become the friend and companion you wanted. He will react to you with all types of behavior: nipping, gnawing at furniture, and just being very playful and impish. He is still very immature, and his nervous system is not fully developed. At this age you must handle him carefully, as how you treat him now will reflect on his behavior patterns. His motor skills are still developing so be patient and loving in your training and discipline.

Around five to six months of age begins the stage of puppy adolescence. The Dalmatian puppy may become quite leggy and awkward looking. Their bodies are filling out but their legs seem to grow much faster, making them to look somewhat like a little giraffe. Spotting also becomes much more defined and darker. Some Dalmatian's spots, when very young, have a gray appearance, but as they become older the black and liver colors become more pronounced. The coat begins to thicken and will start to acquire the coarseness that the dog will display as an adult.

By seven months of age, you will have a good idea how your dog will look as an adult. His size and character are fairly well established and his spotting

Nylafloss® proves to be great fun for dogs of all ages while acting as a dental floss to remove plaque.

is clear. His puppy assertiveness is turning into a more confident and mature attitude. He has now become a close family member and has a good idea of what is acceptable and unacceptable behavior. By now he should be basically housetrained. His motor control will allow him to hold his urine and stool until the proper time,

At five to six months of age Dalmatian adolescents appear quite leggy.

although there may still be accidents. His stomach is larger so he can now handle two larger meals a day rather than the three or four smaller meals of a puppy. He has his permanent teeth and hopefully his chewing phase has subsided.

By the time he is ten to 12 months of age, your Dalmatian will have reached total maturity. Sexual maturity will also be established. A bitch will come into season anytime between six to 12 months. If you have a male, he is usually ready and willing to engage in sexual relations with a bitch when he is a few months old; however, he is incapable of impregnating a bitch until he is between eight to nine months of age. A male dog will often try "mounting" pillows, legs, and a variety of other items, which only shows that he is becoming sexually mature.

By one year of age, the dog is physically mature, but not totally emotionally mature. He still has a lot of learning to do and will still act, at many times, like a puppy. Please be patient, kind, and loving to your dog throughout his life no matter what trouble he might get into. Remember he is only a dog and cannot tell what you want of him unless you have properly prepared him for his role in society.

DAILY CARE of Your Dalmatian

This poem was written by "A Dog's Friend" in Kansas City, MO.

A Dog's Plea

Treat me kindly, my beloved friend, for no heart in all the world is more grateful for kindness than the loving heart of me.

Do not break my spirit with a stick, for though I might lick your hand between blows, your patience and understanding will more quickly teach me things you would have me learn.

Speak to me often, for your voice is the world's sweetest music, as you must know by the fierce wagging of my tail when your footstep falls upon my waiting ear.

Please take me inside when it is cold and wet, for I am a domesticated animal, no longer accustomed to bitter elements. I ask no greater glory than the privilege of sitting at your feet beside the hearth.

Keep my pan filled with fresh water, for I cannot tell you when I suffer thirst.

Feed me clean food that I may stay well, to romp and play and do your bidding, to walk by your side, and stand ready, willing and able to protect you with my life, should your life be in danger.

And my friend, when I am very old, and I no longer enjoy good health, hearing and sight, do not make heroic efforts to keep me going. I am not having fun. Please see that my trusting life is taken gently. I shall leave this earth knowing with the last breath I draw that my fate was always safest in your hands.

FEEDING

There are many different opinions on the feeding of puppies and dogs. Puppies require a totally different schedule and routine than do adults. Since they are growing, their stomachs cannot hold as much at one time, and their digestive systems are much more sensitive than that of an adult dog. Any foreign

Puppies require a totally different feeding schedule than do adults.

substance can cause a puppy great distress, including vomiting and diarrhea. The same substance in an adult dog can have no effect at all.

A puppy's delicate stomach can easily be upset by any change in its diet.

Puppies between eight weeks and six months require three smaller meals per day. A good- quality puppy kibble mixed with warm water is all

your puppy needs. Always purchase the kibble the breeder has the puppy on, so as not to cause any upset in his delicate little system. With the research still ongoing in the protein and stone problem in Dalmatians, it is recommended you use a low-protein kibble for both puppies and adults.

A good-quality puppy kibble mixed with warm water fed three times a day is all the food your puppy needs to grow properly.

Puppy development differs the same as that of a growing child. Some puppies around the age of four months will only require two meals per day. You can judge this by carefully observing your puppy's eating habits. Dalmatians are usually known to have good appetites and are usually not picky eaters. Do not make them finicky by adding all sorts of supplements.

A young puppy should be given his food and allowed to eat for about 15 to 20 minutes undisturbed. Remove the leftover food after that time. If he does not eat at one meal, he will eat at the next one. He will soon learn to eat at the next meal, as he does not want to go hungry. *Do not* leave food around all day with free access for the dog—this will only cause severe eating problems and an unhealthy, obese animal.

Research has shown that the larger- to middle-sized breeds, such as the Dalmatian, benefit from two equal meals a day after the age of six months. Adult dogs should be fed a good commercial kibble that is low in protein twice daily. Mix the kibble with warm water to moisten it. You can add a teaspoonful or two of a canned food to give your adult dog a little change of pace to his daily meal and continue his healthy appetite.

It is advised to provide variety to your dog's diet or else your dogs may go looking for something without you.

With the growth of the dog food industry and the research they continue to do, the quality of dog food has increased so much that all the old home mixtures are no longer necessary or healthy. Many mixtures used years ago

have been proven to do more harm than good. Leave the dog food to the pros.

Be sure to always purchase a very good-quality kibble, both puppy and adult. Do not let price be your criteria for the brand of dog food you use. A better dog food will always be a little more expensive, but with the health of your animal at stake it is well worth it. Also be sure to check to see what food your puppy was on when he left the breeder. Likewise if you are acquiring an adult dog, do not change his food immediately. It must be a slow process. A drastic change for any dog, young or old, could cause all sorts of digestive upsets.

Besides good food, the most important thing you can give your Dalmatian puppy is fresh, cool water.

Besides good food, the most important thing you can give to your dog is *fresh* water. He must have this available at *all* times, except during housebreaking (when it is monitored). Water should be kept clean and fresh, with easy access for your animal. Stainless steel bowls will help to keep the water cool. Many breeders also recommend stainless steel bowls for feeding, as they can be kept sanitary. Word of caution: *do not overfeed*! A healthy and happy dog is *not* a fat dog.

GROOMING

Grooming of the Dalmatian is quick and easy. It should be done on a daily basis, take only a few minutes of your time, and will keep your dog in excellent condition. Begin grooming your puppy daily so he will be accustomed to his grooming time and learn to enjoy it.

If you give your Dalmatian a good-quality kibble mix, he will patiently wait for it at feeding times.

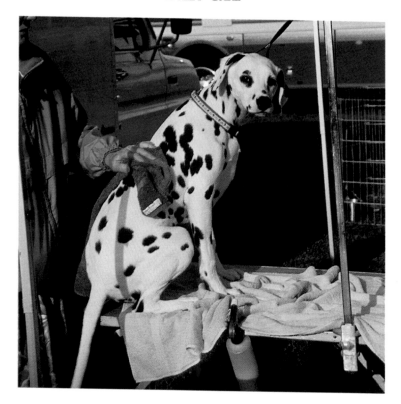

The Dalmatian is basically odor-free and his short coat only needs a light brushing to be kept clean. He will also keep himself clean by his licking. Purchase a good natural-bristle brush, a shedding blade, and a horsehair mitt. Begin by using the shedding blade very gently, as the Dal's coat is thin. Follow up with the natural-bristle brush, brushing with the coat and then against the coat. Finish off with the horsehair mitt, which will remove any loose hair left from the previous tools.

Your Dalmatian's coat requires little grooming; however, a daily brushing will help to keep it shiny and healthy looking.

Bathing should be done on a minimum. I have house dogs that are only bathed twice a year and are as clean as a whistle. If you do bathe your dog, be sure to use a mild shampoo. Begin at his head and work your way down his body. Be sure to keep the water out of his ears and eyes and remember to go down his legs and tail. A good implement while soaping him is a rubber curry brush. Brush him with it while he is wet to loosen any dead hair. After his bath, be sure to dry him very well with a soft towel or blow dryer. Some dogs love the blow dryer and some resist it so do what is best for your dog.

Nails should be kept short. Long nails can cause a dog's feet to splay, meaning spread out. Use a good-quality clipper. Hold the dog's paw firmly, but not too tightly as to frighten him. Be sure to stay away from the quick, the pink area of the nail, and cut just below the hook area. Another device that can be used in nail cutting is the grinder. This grinds the nails down rather than cutting them. Be sure to start cutting your dog's nails at an early age so that he will become accustomed to this procedure.

Using an electric file prevents possible injury.

Ears should only be cleaned on the inner surface. *Do not* try to go deep into your dog's ear canal, as this can cause damage to the inner ear. Use a soft cloth or cotton ball wet with a mild solution of soap and water or an over-the-counter ear cleaner for dogs. Gently wipe the ear surface clean. If your dog is shaking his head frequently, or there is an odor coming from his ear, this may indicate an infection and should be checked by your veterinarian. Dalmatians have large, floppy ears with deep ear canals, and an occasional ear problem is no cause for alarm.

Dalmatians do not have any eye discharge and they don't drool into wrinkled faces or long hair, which help to keep them clean and odor-free. There is no cutting or trimming to be done on this breed except the whiskers. These are removed around the muzzle and over the eyes. It should only be done if the dog is being shown, not on pet dogs.

Teeth should be checked regularly for any irregularities or sore areas of the gums. If tartar does develop, or you see a problem, take your dog to the veterinarian for a complete cleaning and scaling. Tartar only develops after the dog has matured.

Whenever you groom your Dalmatian, always be sure to check him over for any sores, cuts, or skin irritations. Be aware of any irregularities you may find and care for them immediately. Many a minor problem, if treated immediately, will eliminate a more serious condition.

Dalmatians bore from constant repetition— keep training sessions short and interesting to avoid a yawning Dal!

With very little time involved, your Dalmatian will be an easy dog to care for. A dog that is not only fed well but is groomed well and on a regular basis will be a happier dog.

TRAINING AND OBEDIENCE

Training, whether it is formal obedience or informal basic commands, is a very important part of any dog's life. The training you do will decide whether you will have an enjoyable companion or a misbehaved dog that is a bother to everyone.

Training your puppy can begin as early as two months in what is called

No one enjoys a misbehaved dog. It is your responsibility as an owner to train your Dalmatian.

Puppy Kindergarten, which is a small group of puppies that are being exposed to each other and various new situations. It is not formal training but a gradual exposure to new situations and people. Puppy Kindergarten is basic, and usually the first experience that most puppies have in socialization. It is highly recommended to all puppy buyers.

Formal obedience training should not begin until around five to six months of age. This does not mean that you should not be teaching the basic commands, such as no, come, sit and a very short stay. Puppies have a very short attention span when they are very young, not unlike that of a small child. Forced or harsh training can ruin a puppy and will break his spirit for life. A young dog exposed to severe punishment at an early age is likely to be a shy, scared dog for the rest of his lifetime.

By six months formal obedience training can commence. Do not expect in one or two lessons that your dog will know what you want. It is a slow, gradual, and repetitive process. With gentle and patient commands and constant repetition, your puppy will soon master all that you could expect and then some.

The Dalmatian has a very retentive memory. Once a command is learned, he will respond with much

Once a command is learned by a Dalmatian, he will respond with much eagerness: he is a dog that wishes to please.

eagerness, as he is a dog that wishes to please. Always make your training sessions fun. A great deal of praise is required to establish a desirable routine with your dog.

Dalmatians do very well in the obedience ring. Their keen memory and their eagerness to please their handlers make them great candidates for formal training. There are two special obedience events that the Dalmatian is exceptionally suited for. The first is tracking, which involves the dog

Tracking equipment—harness and 40-foot lead, flags, assorted articles including a wallet, and dark glove. For the handler— boots, canteen and pack to carry articles and clothes pins for marking turns.

This Dalmatian seems to have no trouble clearing the bar at an agility trial.

following a marked track. The use of the sense of smell, or scent, is what is the major factor in this trial. Dalmatians enjoy this exercise, as they were once used for hunting.

Dalmatians derive from gundogs and retrievers—many take to the water effortlessly.

The second specialty event is the Road Trial. Coaching is a breed-specific event sanctioned by the Dalmatian Club of America. This is a revived event in the art of "Coaching," which the Dalmatian was once known for. The regulations state, "The purpose of the road trial is to demonstrate the use of the purebred Dalmatian as a companion to man in the role that they had been bred to perform." There are three basic areas in road trials: obedience, a novice routine with the handler on horseback; speed, to show the dog's speed capability; and endurance, to demonstrate that Dalmatians were bred for and can handle long endurance trials. Two distances are offered: one is 12.5 miles, and the other is the Road Trial Excellent, which is 25 miles.

Show training is not your regular obedience training. The dog must have some basic behavior training but also know the formal routine of the obedience ring. If you are interested in showing your dog in the breed ring, you must begin training very early. A seven-week-old puppy should be "set up" in a show pose for a few minutes several times a day. Always attend a good show-handling class, for there is as much for you to learn as there is for your dog.

Breed showing requires a dog to be highly disciplined in the show ring. The judge will "go over" your dog very carefully, touching legs, ears, tail, torso, and testicles. He will also carefully examine your dog's teeth. A dog must stand still for whatever examination he is given. He must be willing to accept other dogs close behind him and close in front of him.

Winning Best in Show requires a dog to be of unquestionably superior quality as well as highly disciplined in the show ring.

BEST IN
SHOW
GREATER PHILADELPHIA
DOG FANCIERS
JUNE 1979

This is all accomplished by a slow and gradual training process, rewarded with a large amount of praise.

EXERCISE

Exercise is a vital part of every dog's life, from a very young puppy to an older dog. To keep your dog alert, vibrant, and healthy, you must provide him with plenty of fresh air and exercise. As a dog owner you are totally responsible for your dog's health and well being, and exercise plays a key role in the life of a Dalmatian. Dalmatians were coaching dogs used to running and exercising for hours. They were built for endurance. In reality, today's Dalmatians cannot run beside a carriage for exercise and enjoyment, so proper exercise must fill this need.

Dalmatians love to run, but in today's busy society, in most areas, a dog may not be allowed to run free because of both legal and safety reasons. Be sure to take your dog on long walks if you are a city dweller, and hopefully you can find a park where you will be able to allow him to run more freely on a long lead. It is unsafe to let even a well-trained dog run free, as there is always the fear of unknown dangers popping up, especially automobiles.

Suburbanites usually have the benefit of a backyard. This should be totally fenced in, affording your dog lots of free-running time, or a kennel area should be built to accommodate him. If you do put up a kennel area, be sure it is large enough for a good run and at least six feet high, as Dals love to jump. Even though you may have a fenced-in area, please take your dog on walks. This will help to continue the companionship you have begun to develop.

Country folk usually have the privilege of safer areas, and their dog will be allowed a little more freedom; however, care must always be taken for his safety.

Dalmatians love to play! Playing Frisbee™, fetching a ball, and playing tug of war will keep him happy and help give him the exercise and attention he needs. I know many of our Dals also enjoy a good swim, whether it is in a backyard pool or in a nearby pond or lake. Many owners who jog also enjoy taking their Dal with them, just be sure you do not overwork your dog. You may also want to have your Dalmatian run next to you on your bicycle for short periods of time. This is excellent exercise and teaches him to stay close by your side. It is a form of modern-day coaching. Be sure to do this on a limited basis, do not overdo the exercise.

A note of caution, do not begin your puppy on a vigorous exercise routine. A puppy is developing his bones and muscles, and must slowly be introduced to long walks and runs. As he grows, so will his ability to handle more exercising with and without you.

Be sure to moderate your Dalmatian's exercise routine in the hot summer months and the cold winter ones.

The Dalmatian is a muscular dog and just as people who receive no exercise become listless and out of shape, so will your Dalmatian. Be sure to moderate his exercise routine in the hot summer months and the cold winter ones.

With today's economy, most families have little time at home during the day, due to work or school. The dog is usually "home alone," all day, either crated or in a special room provided for him. That is why it is even more important to give him his daily run as much as possible. Be sure you give him as much quality time as you can when you are at home with your Dal. The proper care, diet, exercise, veterinarian check ups, and love will reward you with a very healthy and happy companion for a long time.

SPORT of Purebred Dogs

Welcome to the exciting and sometimes frustrating sport of dogs. No doubt you are trying to learn more about dogs or you wouldn't be deep into this book. This section covers the basics that may entice you, further your knowledge and help you to understand the dog world. If you decide to give showing, obedience or any other dog activities a try, then I suggest you seek further help from the appropriate source.

Dog showing has been a very popular sport for a long time and has been taken quite seriously by some. Others only enjoy it as a hobby.

The Kennel Club in England was formed in 1859, the American Kennel Club was established in 1884 and the Canadian Kennel Club was formed in 1888.

This is Lyco's Dream Girl bred by the author Helen W. Shue. Showing is an exciting and often frustrating dog sport, but a win makes it all worth while.

The purpose of these clubs was to register purebred dogs and maintain their Stud Books. In the beginning, the concept of registering dogs was not readily accepted. More than 36 million dogs have been enrolled in the AKC Stud Book since its inception in 1888. Presently the kennel clubs not only register dogs but adopt and enforce rules and regulations governing dog shows, obedience trials and field trials. Over the years they have fostered and encouraged interest in the health and welfare of the purebred dog. They routinely donate funds to veterinary research for study on genetic disorders.

Below are the addresses of the kennel clubs in the United States, Great Britain and Canada.

The American Kennel Club
51 Madison Avenue
New York, NY 10010
(Their registry is located at: 5580 Centerview Drive, STE 200, Raleigh, NC 27606-3390)

WINNERS

SUSSEX HILLS
SHKC
KENNEL CLUB

AUGUST
30,
1992

DAVE ASHBEY

Dalmatian coming over the A-frame at agility trial practice.

The Kennel Club
1 Clarges Street
Piccadilly, London, WIY 8AB, England

The Canadian Kennel Club
111 Eglinton Avenue
East Toronto, Ontario M6S 4V7
Canada

Today there are numerous activities that are enjoyable for both the dog and the handler. Some of the activities include conformation showing, obedience competition, agility, the Canine Good Citizen Certificate, and a wide range of instinct tests that vary from breed to breed. Where you start depends upon your goals which early on may not be readily apparent.

PUPPY KINDERGARTEN

Every puppy will benefit from this class. PKT is the foundation for all future dog activities from conformation to "couch potatoes." Pet owners should make an effort to attend even if they never expect to show their dog. The class is designed for puppies about three months of age with graduation at approximately five months of age. All the puppies will be in the same age group and, even though some may be a little unruly, there should not be any real problem. This class will teach the puppy some beginning obedience. As in all obedience classes the owner learns how to train his own dog. The PKT class gives the puppy the opportunity to interact with other puppies in the same age group and exposes him to strangers, which is very important. Some dogs grow up with behavior problems, one of them being fear of strangers. As you can see, there can be much to gain from this class.

Puppy Kindergarten class will give your Dalmatian puppy the opportunity to interact with other puppies of his age group.

There are some basic obedience exercises that every dog should learn. Some of these can be started with puppy kindergarten.

Sit

One way of teaching the sit is to have your dog on your left side with the leash in your right hand, close to the collar. Pull up on the leash and at the same time reach around his hindlegs with your left hand and tuck them in. As you are doing this say, "Beau, sit." Always use the dog's name when you give an active command. Some owners like to use a treat holding it over the dog's head. The dog will need to sit to get the treat. Encourage the dog to hold the sit for a few seconds, which will eventually be the beginning of the Sit/Stay. Depending on how cooperative

he is, you can rub him under the chin or stroke his back. It is a good time to establish eye contact.

Down

Sit the dog on your left side and kneel down beside him with the leash in your right hand. Reach over him with your left hand and grasp his left foreleg. With your right hand, take his right foreleg and pull his legs forward while you say, "Beau, down." If he tries to get up, lean on his shoulder to encourage him to stay down. It will relax your dog if you stroke his back while he is down. Try to encourage him to stay down for a few seconds as preparation for the Down/Stay.

Heel

The definition of heeling is the dog walking under control at your left heel. Your puppy will learn controlled walking in the puppy kindergarten class, which will eventually lead to heeling. The command is "Beau, heel," and you start off briskly with your left foot. Your leash is in your right hand and your left hand is holding it about half way down. Your left

The "down" command will make encounters with people more comfortable for both you, your Dal and your friend.

hand should be able to control the leash and there should be a little slack in it. You want him to walk with you with your leg somewhere between his nose and his shoulder. You need to encourage him to stay with you, not forging (in front of you) or lagging behind you. It is best to keep him on a fairly short lead. Do not allow the lead to become tight. It is far better to give him a little jerk when necessary and remind him to heel. When you come to a halt, be prepared physically to make him sit. It takes practice to become coordinated. There are excellent books on training that you may wish to purchase. Your instructor should be able to recommend one for you.

When training your dog, it is best to work on a short lead that cannot become too tight.

97

Recall

This quite possibly is the most important exercise you will ever teach. It should be a pleasant experience. The puppy may learn to do random recalls while being attached to a long line such as a clothes line. Later the exercise will start with the dog sitting and staying until called. The command is "Beau, come." Let your command be happy. You want your dog to come willingly and faithfully. The recall could save his life if he sneaks out the door. In practicing the recall, let him jump on you or touch you before you reach for him. If he is shy, then kneel down to his level. Reaching for the insecure dog could frighten him, and he may not be willing to come again in the future. Lots of praise and a treat would be in order whenever you do a recall. Under no circumstances should you ever correct your dog when he has come to you. Later in formal obedience your dog will be required to sit in front of you after recalling and then go to heel position.

CONFORMATION

Conformation showing is our oldest dog show sport. This type of showing is based on the dog's appearance—that is his structure, movement and attitude. When considering this type of showing, you need to be aware of your breed's standard and be able to evaluate your dog compared to that standard. The breeder of your puppy or other experienced breeders would be good sources for such an evaluation. Puppies can go through lots of changes over a period of time. I always say most puppies start out as promising

Conformation showing allows an owner and/or handler to see how well their dog matches up to the standard.

hopefuls and then after maturing may be disappointing as show candidates. Even so this should not deter them from being excellent pets.

Usually conformation training classes are offered by the local kennel or obedience clubs. These are excellent places for training puppies. The puppy should be able to walk on a lead before entering such a class. Proper ring procedure and

Buying a puppy, even of champion lines, is always a roll of the dice.

Before you even enroll in obedience class, be sure your puppy is accustomed to walking on a lead.

technique for posing (stacking) the dog will be demonstrated as well as gaiting the dog. Usually certain patterns are used in the ring such as the triangle or the "L." Conformation class, like the PKT class, will give your youngster the opportunity to socialize with different breeds of dogs and humans too.

It takes some time to learn the routine of conformation showing. Usually one starts at the puppy matches which may be AKC Sanctioned or Fun Matches. These matches are generally for puppies from two or three months to a year old, and there may be classes for the adult over the age of 12 months. Similar to point shows, the classes are divided by sex and after completion of the classes in that breed or variety, the class winners compete for Best of Breed or Variety. The winner goes on to compete in the Group and the Group winners compete for Best in Match. No championship points are awarded for match wins.

Best of Breed winners go on to compete for Group first and then for Best in Show or Match.

A few matches can be great training for puppies even though there is no intention to go on showing. Matches enable the puppy to meet new people and be handled by a stranger—the judge. It is also a change of environment, which broadens the horizon for both dog and handler. Matches and other dog activities boost the confidence of the handler and especially the younger handlers.

Earning an AKC championship is built on a point system, which is different from Great Britain. To become an AKC Champion of Record the dog must earn 15 points. The number of points earned each time depends upon the number of dogs in competition. The number of points available at each show depends upon the breed, its sex and the location of the show. The United States is divided into ten AKC zones. Each zone has its own set of points. The purpose of the zones is to try to equalize the points available from breed to breed and area to area. The AKC adjusts the point scale annually.

The dog show world is a busy life. Sometimes owners and handlers must travel great distances within short periods of time to arrive at the next show.

The number of points that can be won at a show are between one and five. Three-, four- and five-point wins are considered majors. Not only does the dog need 15 points won under three different judges, but those points must include two majors under two different judges. Canada also works on a point system but majors are not required.

Each handler is responsible for his/her own dog's actions while in the ring.

Dogs always show before bitches. The classes available to those seeking points are: Puppy (which may be divided into 6 to 9 months and 9 to 12 months); 12 to 18 months; Novice; Bred-by-Exhibitor; American-bred; and Open. The class winners of the same sex of each breed or variety compete against each other for Winners Dog and Winners Bitch. A Reserve Winners Dog and Reserve Winners Bitch are also awarded but do not carry any points unless the Winners win is disallowed by AKC. The Winners Dog and Bitch compete with the specials (those dogs that have attained championship) for Best of Breed or Variety, Best of Winners and Best of Opposite

Sex. It is possible to pick up an extra point or even a major if the points are higher for the defeated winner than those of Best of Winners. The latter would get the higher total from the defeated winner.

At an all-breed show, each Best of Breed or Variety winner will go on to his respective Group and then the Group winners will compete against each other for Best in Show. There are seven Groups: Sporting, Hounds, Working, Terriers, Toys, Non-Sporting and Herding. Obviously there are no Groups at speciality shows (those shows that have only one breed or a show such as the American Spaniel Club's Flushing Spaniel Show, which is for all flushing spaniel breeds).

Earning a championship in England is somewhat different since they do not have a point system. Challenge Certificates *Earning a championship in England is different than in America and Canada.* are awarded if the judge feels the dog is deserving regardless of the number of dogs in competition. A dog must earn three Challenge Certificates under three different judges, with at least one of these Certificates being won after the age of 12

months. Competition is very strong and entries may be higher than they are in the U.S. The Kennel Club's Challenge Certificates are only available at Championship Shows.

In England, The Kennel Club regulations require that certain dogs, Border Collies and Gundog breeds, qualify in a working capacity (i.e., obedience or field trials) before becoming a full Champion. If they do not qualify in the working aspect, then they are designated a Show Champion, which is equivalent to the AKC's Champion of Record. A Gundog may be granted the title of Field Trial Champion (FT Ch) if it passes all the tests in the field but would also have to qualify in conformation before becoming a full Champion. A Border Collie that earns the title of Obedience Champion (Ob Ch) must also qualify in the conformation ring before becoming a Champion.

The U.S. doesn't have a designation full Champion but does award for Dual and Triple Champions. The Dual Champion must be a Champion of Record, and either Champion Tracker, Herding Champion, Obedience Trial Champion or Field Champion. Any dog that has been awarded the titles of Champion of Record, and any two of the following: Champion Tracker, Herding Champion, Obedience Trial Champion or Field Champion, may be designated as a Triple Champion.

The shows in England seem to put more emphasis on breeder judges than those in the U.S. There is much competition within the breeds. Therefore the quality of the individual breeds should be very good. In the United States we

Although the United States and England differ in their manner of showing, both are very competitive. Overall dog shows are more popular in England then in the U.S.

tend to have more "all around
judges" (those that judge
multiple breeds) and use the
breeder judges at the specialty
shows. Breeder judges are more
familiar with their own breed
since they are actively breeding
that breed or did so at one time.
Americans emphasize Group and
Best in Show wins and promote
them accordingly.

*Ch. Sugar Frost Flying
Parson owned by Janet
Ashbey is Winners Dog at a
local show.*

It is my understanding that the
shows in England can be very
large and extend over several
days, with the Groups being
scheduled on different days. I believe there is only one all-
breed show in the U.S. that extends over two days, the
Westminster Kennel Club Show. In our country we have
cluster shows, where several different clubs will use the same
show site over consecutive days.

Westminster Kennel Club is our most prestigious show
although the entry is limited to 2500. In recent years, entry
has been limited to Champions. This show is more formal than
the majority of the shows with the judges wearing formal
attire and the handlers fashionably dressed. In most instances
the quality of the dogs is superb. After all, it is a show of
Champions. It is a good show to study the AKC registered
breeds and is by far the most exciting—especially since it is
televised! WKC is one of the few shows in this country that is
still benched. This means the dog must be in his benched area
during the show hours except when he is being groomed, in
the ring, or being exercised.

Typically, the handlers are very particular about their
appearances. They are careful not to wear something that will
detract from their dog but will perhaps enhance it. American
ring procedure is quite formal compared to that of other
countries. I remember being reprimanded by a judge because
I made a suggestion to a friend holding my second dog outside
the ring. I certainly could have used more discretion so I
would not call attention to myself. There is a certain etiquette
expected between the judge and exhibitor and among the

other exhibitors. Of course it is not always the case but the judge is supposed to be polite, not engaging in small talk or even acknowledging that he knows the handler. I understand that there is a more informal and relaxed atmosphere at the shows in other countries. For instance, the dress code is more casual. I can see where this might be more fun for the exhibitor and especially for the novice. This country is very handler-oriented in many of the breeds. It is true, in most instances, that the experienced professional handler can present the dog better and will have a feel for what a judge likes.

Professional handlers can present a dog better than most owners.

In England, Crufts is The Kennel Club's own show and is most assuredly the largest dog show in the world. They've been known to have an entry of nearly 20,000, and the show lasts four days. Entry is only gained by qualifying through winning in specified classes at another Championship Show. Westminster is strictly conformation, but Crufts exhibitors and spectators enjoy not only conformation but obedience, agility and a multitude of exhibitions as well. Obedience was admitted in 1957 and agility in 1983.

If you are handling your own dog, please give some consideration to your apparel. For sure the dress code at matches is more informal than the point shows. However, you should wear something a little more appropriate than beach attire or ragged jeans and bare feet. If you check out the handlers and see what is presently fashionable, you'll catch on. Men usually dress with a shirt and tie and a nice sports coat. Whether you are male or female, you will want to wear comfortable clothes and shoes. You need to be able to run with your dog and you certainly don't want to take a chance of falling and hurting yourself. Heaven forbid, if nothing else, you'll

Pictured here are two multi-titled champions of the 1990 World Dog Show, a Dalmatian and an Old English Sheepdog.

It is important that handlers wear comfortable clothes, preferably with pockets for bait, and sensible shoes.

upset your dog. Women usually wear a dress or two-piece outfit, preferably with pockets to carry bait, comb, brush, etc. In this case men are the lucky ones with all their pockets. Ladies, think about where your dress will be if you need to kneel on the floor and also think about running. Does it allow freedom to do so?

Years ago, after toting around all the baby paraphernalia, I found toting the dog and necessities a breeze. You need to take along dog; crate; ex pen (if you use one); extra newspaper; water pail and water; all required grooming equipment, including hair dryer and extension cord; table; chair for you; bait for dog and lunch for you and friends; and, last but not least, clean up materials, such as plastic bags, paper towels, and perhaps a bath towel and some shampoo—

just in case. Don't forget your entry confirmation and directions to the show.

If you are showing in obedience, then you will want to wear pants. Many of our top obedience handlers wear pants that are color-coordinated with their dogs. The philosophy is that imperfections in the black dog will be less obvious next to your black pants.

Whether you are showing in conformation, Junior Showmanship or obedience, you need to watch the clock and be sure you are not late. It is customary to pick up your conformation armband a few minutes before the start of the class. They will not wait for you and if you are on the show grounds and not in the ring, you will upset everyone. It's a little more complicated picking up your obedience armband if you show later in the class. If you have not picked up your armband and they get to your number, you may not be allowed to show. It's best to pick up your armband early, but then you may show earlier than expected if other handlers don't pick up. Customarily all conflicts should be discussed with the judge prior to the start of the class.

Dress to complement your Dalmatian. Choose a vivid solid color—and never wear polka dots!

Junior Showmanship

The Junior Showmanship Class is a wonderful way to build self confidence even if there are no aspirations of staying with the dog-show game later in life. Frequently, Junior Showmanship becomes the background of those who become successful exhibitors/handlers in the future. In some instances it is taken very seriously, and success is measured in terms of wins. The Junior Handler is judged solely on his ability and skill in presenting his dog. The dog's conformation is not to be

considered by the judge. Even so the condition and grooming of the dog may be a reflection upon the handler.

Usually the matches and point shows include different classes. The Junior Handler's dog may be entered in a breed or obedience class and even shown by another person in that class. Junior Showmanship classes are usually divided by age. The age is determined by the handler's age on the day of the show. The classes are:

Novice Junior for those at least ten and under 14 years of age who at time of entry closing have not won three first places in a Novice Class at a licensed or member show.

Novice Senior for those at least 14 and under 18 years of age who at the time of entry closing have not won three first places in a Novice Class at a licensed or member show.

Open Junior for those at least ten and under 14 years of age who at the time of entry closing have won at least three first places in a Novice Junior Showmanship Class at a licensed or member show with competition present.

The Canine Good Citizen program is sponsored by the AKC to encourage dog owners to provide basic training for their dogs.

Open Senior for those at least 14 and under 18 years of age who at time of entry closing have won at least three first places in a Novice Junior Showmanship Class at a licensed or member show with competition present.

Junior Handlers must include their AKC Junior Handler number on each show entry. This needs to be obtained from the AKC.

The experience and success of obedience trials bring the bonus of a well-mannered companion.

CANINE GOOD CITIZEN

The AKC sponsors a program to encourage dog owners to train their dogs. Local clubs perform the pass/fail tests, and dogs who pass are awarded a Canine Good Citizen Certificate. Proof of vaccination is required at the time of participation. The

111

test includes:

1. Accepting a friendly stranger.
2. Sitting politely for petting.
3. Appearance and grooming.
4. Walking on a loose leash.
5. Walking through a crowd.
6. Sit and down on command/staying in place.
7. Coming when called.
8. Reaction to another dog.
9. Reactions to distractions.
10. Supervised separation.

If more effort was made by pet owners to accomplish these exercises, fewer dogs would be cast off to the humane shelter.

OBEDIENCE

Obedience is necessary, without a doubt, but it can also become a wonderful hobby or even an obsession. In my opinion, obedience classes and competition can provide wonderful companionship, not only with your dog but with your classmates or fellow competitors. It is always gratifying to discuss your dog's problems with others who have had similar experiences. The AKC acknowledged Obedience around 1936, and it has changed tremendously even though many of the exercises are basically the same. Today, obedience competition is just that—very competitive. Even so, it is possible for every obedience exhibitor to come home a winner (by earning qualifying scores) even though he/she may not earn a placement in the class.

Dalmatian executing the broad jump at an obedience trial.

Most of the obedience titles are awarded after earning three qualifying scores (legs) in the appropriate class under three different judges. These classes offer a perfect score of 200, which is extremely rare. Each of the class exercises has its own point value. A leg is earned after receiving a score of at least 170 and at least 50 percent of the points available in each exercise. The titles are:

Early socialization is important to a puppy's personality and future.

Agility trials are obstacle courses designed to test a dog's intelligence and coordination.

Companion Dog–CD

This is called the Novice Class and the exercises are:

Long sits are part of earning an obedience title.

1. Heel on leash and figure 8 40 points	
2. Stand for examination	30 points
3. Heel free	40 points
4. Recall	30 points
5. Long sit—one minute	30 points
6. Long down—three minutes	30 points
Maximum total score	200 points

Companion Dog Excellent–CDX

This is the Open Class and the exercises are:

1. Heel off leash and figure 8	40 points
2. Drop on recall	30 points
3. Retrieve on flat	20 points
4. Retrieve over high jump	30 points
5. Broad jump	20 points
6. Long sit—three minutes (out of sight)	30 points
7. Long down—five minutes (out of sight)	30 points
Maximum total score	200 points

Utility Dog–UD

The Utility Class exercises are:

1. Signal Exercise	40 points
2. Scent discrimination-Article 1	30 points
3. Scent discrimination-Article 2	30 points
4. Directed retrieve	30 points
5. Moving stand and examination	30 points
6. Directed jumping	40 points
Maximum total score	200 points

After achieving the UD title, you may feel inclined to go after the UDX and/or OTCh. The UDX (Utility Dog Excellent) title went into effect in January 1994. It is not easily attained. The title requires qualifying simultaneously ten times in Open B and Utility B but not necessarily at consecutive shows.

Heeling, both on and off leash, is another part of earning an obedience title.

The OTCh (Obedience Trial Champion) is awarded after the dog has earned his UD and then goes on to earn 100 championship points, a first place in Utility, a first place in Open and another first place in either class.

The placements must be won under three different judges at all-breed obedience trials. The points are determined by the number of dogs competing in the Open B and Utility B classes. The OTCh title precedes the dog's name.

Obedience matches (AKC Sanctioned, Fun, and Show and Go) are usually available. Usually they are sponsored by the local obedience clubs. When preparing an obedience dog for a title, you will find matches very helpful. Fun Matches and Show and Go Matches are more lenient in allowing you to make corrections in the ring. I frequently train (correct) in the ring and inform the judge that I would like to do so and to please mark me "exhibition." This means that I will not be eligible for any prize. This type of training is usually very necessary for the Open and Utility Classes. AKC Sanctioned Obedience Matches do not allow corrections in the ring since they must abide by the AKC Obedience Regulations. If you are interested in showing in obedience, then you should contact AKC for a copy of the Obedience Regulations.

As this Dalmatian flies through the tire jump you can almost hear the crowd cheer. Agility is a spectator sport!

TRACKING

Tracking is officially classified obedience, but I feel it should have its own category. There are three tracking titles available. If all three tracking titles are obtained, then the dog officially becomes a CT (Champion Tracker). The CT will go in front of the dog's name.

A TD may be earned anytime and does not have to follow the other obedience titles. There are many exhibitors that prefer tracking to obedience, and there are others like myself that do both. In my experience with small dogs, I prefer to earn the CD and CDX before attempting tracking. My reasoning is that small dogs are closer to the mat in the obedience rings and therefore it's too easy to put the nose down and sniff. Tracking encourages sniffing. Of course this depends on the dog. I've had some dogs that tracked around the ring and others (TDXs) who wouldn't think of sniffing in the ring.

Tracking Dog–TD

Tracking is designed to test a dog's ability to discriminate scents. A dog must be certified by an AKC tracking judge that he is ready to perform in an AKC test. The AKC can provide the names of tracking judges in your area that you can contact for certification. Depending on where you live, you may have to travel a distance if there is no local tracking judge. The certification track will be equivalent to a regular AKC track. A regulation track must be 440 to 500 yards long with at least two right-angle turns out in the open. The track will be aged 30 minutes to two hours. The handler has two starting flags at the beginning of the track to indicate the direction started. The dog works on a harness and 40-foot lead and must work at least 20 feet in front of the handler. An article (either a dark glove or wallet) will be dropped at the end of the track, and the dog must indicate it but not necessarily retrieve it.

People always ask me what the dog tracks. In my opinion, initially, the beginner on the short-aged track tracks the tracklayer. Eventually the dog learns to track the disturbed vegetation and learns to differentiate between tracks. Getting started with tracking requires reading the AKC regulations and a good book on tracking plus finding other tracking enthusiasts. I like to work on the buddy system. That is—we lay tracks for each other so we can practice blind tracks. It is possible to train on your own, but if you are a beginner, it is a lot more entertaining to track with a buddy. Tracking is my favorite dog sport. It's rewarding seeing the dog use his natural ability.

Tracking Dog Excellent—TDX

The TDX track is 800 to 1000 yards long and is aged three to five hours. There will be five to seven turns. An article is left at the starting flag, and three other articles must be indicated on the track. There is only one flag at the start, so it is a blind start. Approximately one and a half hours after the track is laid, two tracklayers will cross over the track at two different places to test the dog's ability to stay with the original track. There will be at least two obstacles on the track such as a change of cover, fences, creeks, ditches, etc. The dog must have a TD before entering a TDX. There is no certification required for a TDX.

Tracking is a very difficult task for a dog to learn.

Variable Surface Tracking—VST

This test came into effect September 1995. The dog must have a TD earned at least six months prior to entering this test. The track is 600 to 800 yards long and shall have a minimum of three different surfaces. Vegetation shall be included along with two areas devoid of vegetation such as concrete, asphalt, gravel, sand, hard pan or mulch. The areas devoid of vegetation shall comprise at least one-third to one-half of the track. The track is aged three to five hours. There will be four to eight turns and four numbered articles including one leather, one plastic, one metal and one fabric dropped on the track. There is one starting flag. The handler will work at least 10 feet from the dog.

AGILITY

Agility was first introduced by John Varley in England at the Crufts Dog Show, February 1978, but Peter Meanwell, competitor and judge, actually developed the idea. It was officially recognized in the early '80s. Agility is extremely popular in England and Canada and growing in popularity in the U.S. The AKC acknowledged agility in August 1994. Dogs must be at least 12 months of age to be entered. It is a fascinating sport that the dog, handler and spectators enjoy to the utmost. Agility is a spectator sport! The dog performs off lead. The handler either runs with his dog or positions himself on the course and directs his dog with verbal and hand signals over a timed course over or through a variety of obstacles including a time out or pause. One of the main drawbacks to agility is finding a place to train. The obstacles take up a lot of space and it is very time consuming to put up and take down courses.

The titles earned at AKC agility trials are Novice Agility Dog (NAD), Open Agility Dog (OAD), Agility Dog Excellent (ADX), and Master Agility Excellent (MAX). In order to acquire an

The agility ring at the Crufts Dog Show. Agility is extremely popular in England and Canada and is rapidly gaining popularity in the United States.

agility title, a dog must earn a qualifying score in its respective class on three separate occasions under two different judges. The MAX will be awarded after earning ten qualifying scores in the Agility Excellent Class.

PERFORMANCE TESTS

During the last decade the American Kennel Club has promoted performance tests—those events that test the different breeds' natural abilities. This type of event encourages a handler to devote even more time to his dog and retain the natural instincts of his breed heritage. It is an important part of the wonderful world of dogs.

Lure Coursing

For all sighthounds (Afghans, Basenjis, Borzois, Greyhounds, Ibizans, Irish Wolfhounds, Pharaoh Hounds, Rhodesian Ridgebacks, Salukis, Scottish Deerhounds, and Whippets).

Road Trials are present day attempts to revive the breed's coaching instincts. The participant must be at least one year of age, and dogs with limited registration (ILP) are elgible. They chase a lure of three plastic bags and are judged on overall ability, follow, speed, agility and endurance. Like the other AKC

performance tests, lure coursing gives dogs the opportunity to prove themselves at what they were originally bred to do.

Junior Courser (JC) A hound running alone shall receive certification from a judge on one date, and a second certification at a later time, stating the hound completed a 600-yard course with a minimum of four turns. The hound must complete the course with enthusiasm and without interruption.

Senior Courser (SC) Must be elgible to enter the open stake and the hound must run with at least one other hound. Must receive qualifying scores at four AKC-licensed or member trials under two different judges.

Field Championship (FC) Prefix to the hound's name. Must receive 15 championship points including two first placements with three points or more under two different judges.

Earthdog Events

For small terriers (Australian, Bedlington, Border, Cairn, Dandie Dinmont, Fox (Smooth & Wire), Lakeland, Norfolk, Norwich, Scottish, Sealyham, Skye, Welsh, West Highland White and Dachshunds).

Limited registration (ILP) dogs are eligible and all entrants must be at least six months of age. The primary purpose of the small terriers and Dachshunds is to pursue quarry to ground, hold the game, and alert the hunter where to dig, or to bolt. There are two parts to the test: (1) the approach to the quarry and (2) working the quarry. The dog must pass both parts for a Junior Earthdog (JE). The Senior Earthdog (SE) must do a third part—to leave the den on command. The Master Earthdog (ME) is a bit more complicated.

Dalmatians are most notable as coaching dogs.

Hunting Titles

For retrievers, pointing breeds and spaniels. Titles offered are Junior Hunter (JH), Senior Hunter (SH), and Master Hunter (MH).

Flushing Spaniels Their primary purpose is to hunt, find, flush and return birds to hand as quickly as possible in a pleasing and obedient manner. The entrant must be at least six months of age and dogs with limited registration (ILP) are eligible. Game used are pigeons, pheasants, and quail.

Retrievers Limited registration (ILP) retrievers are not eligible to compete in Hunting Tests. The purpose of a Hunting Test for retrievers is to test the merits of and evaluate the abilities of retrievers in the field in order to determine their suitability and ability as hunting companions. They are expected to retrieve any type of game bird, pheasants, ducks, pigeons, guinea hens and quail.

Pointing Breeds Are eligible at six months of age, and dogs with limited registration (ILP) are not permitted. They must show a keen desire to hunt; be bold and independent; have a fast, yet attractive, manner of hunting; and demonstrate intelligence not only in seeking objectives but also in the ability to find game. They must establish point, and in the more advanced tests they need to be steady to wing and must remain in

The Dalmatian is used by hunters for retrieving, birding and pack hunting.

position until the bird is shot or they are released.

A Senior Hunter must retrieve. A Master Hunter must honor. The judges and the marshal are permitted to ride horseback during the test.

Herding Titles

For all Herding breeds and Rottweilers and Samoyeds.

Entrants must be at least nine months of age and dogs with limited registration (ILP) are eligible. The Herding program is divided into Testing and Trial sections. The goal is to demonstrate proficiency in herding livestock in diverse situations. The titles offered are Herding Started (HS), Herding Intermediate (HI), and Herding Excellent (HX). Upon completion of the HX a Herding Championship may be earned after accumulating 15 championship points.

The above information has been taken from the AKC Guidelines for the appropriate events.

Schutzhund

The German word "Schutzhund" translated to English means "Protection Dog." It is a fast growing competitive sport in the United States and has been popular in England since the early 1900s. Schutzhund was originally a test to determine which German Shepherds were quality dogs for breeding in Germany. It gives us the ability to test our dogs for correct temperament and working ability. Like every other dog sport, it requires teamwork between the handler and the dog.

Schutzhund training and showing involves three phases: Tracking, Obedience and Protection. There are three SchH levels: SchH I (novice), SchH II (intermediate), and SchH III (advanced). Each title becomes progressively more difficult. The handler and dog start out in each phase with 100 points. Points are deducted as errors are incurred. A total perfect score is 300, and for a dog and handler to earn a title he must earn at least 70 points in tracking and obedience and at least 80 points in protection. Today many different breeds participate successfully in Schutzhund.

General Information

Obedience, tracking and agility allow the purebred dog with an Indefinite Listing Privilege (ILP) number or a limited registration to be exhibited and earn titles. Application must be made to the AKC for an ILP number.

The American Kennel Club publishes a monthly *events* magazine that is part of the *Gazette*, their official journal for the sport of purebred dogs. The *Events* section lists upcoming shows and the secretary or superintendent for them. The majority of the conformation shows in the U.S. are overseen by licensed superintendents. Generally the entry closing date is approximately two-and-a-half weeks before the actual show. Point shows are fairly expensive, while the match shows cost about one third of the point show entry fee. Match shows usually take entries the day of the show but some are pre-entry. The best way to find match show information is through your local kennel club. Upon asking, the AKC can provide you with a list of superintendents, and you can write and ask to be put on their mailing lists.

Practice rings for Utility training can be set up in fields or nearby parks.

Obedience trial and tracking test information is available through the AKC. Frequently these events are not superintended, but put on by the host club. Therefore you would make the entry with the event's secretary.

As you have read, there are numerous activities you can share with your dog. Regardless what you do, it does take teamwork. Your dog can only benefit from your attention and training. I hope this chapter has enlightened you and hope, if nothing else, you will attend a show here and there. Perhaps you will start with a puppy kindergarten class, and who knows where it may lead!

HEALTH CARE

Veterinary medicine has become far more sophisticated than what was available to our ancestors. This can be attributed to the increase in household pets and consequently the demand for better care for them. Also human medicine has become far more complex. Today diagnostic testing in veterinary medicine parallels human diagnostics. Because of better technology we can expect our pets to live healthier lives thereby increasing their life spans.

THE FIRST CHECK UP

Your pet's health should always be an important factor. Pet owners of today are quite lucky because improved technology allows us to expect our pets to live longer.

You will want to take your new puppy/dog in for its first check up within 48 to 72 hours after acquiring it. Many breeders strongly recommend this check up and so do the humane shelters. A puppy/dog can appear healthy but it may have a serious problem that is not apparent to the layman. Most pets have some type of a minor flaw that may never cause a real problem.

Unfortunately if he/she should have a serious problem, you will want to consider the consequences of keeping the pet and the attachments that will be formed, which may be broken prematurely. Keep in mind there are many healthy dogs looking for good homes.

This first check up is a good time to establish yourself with the veterinarian and learn the office policy regarding their hours and how they handle emergencies. Usually the breeder or another conscientious pet owner is a good reference for locating a capable veterinarian. You should be aware that not all veterinarians give the same quality of service. Please do not make your selection on the least expensive clinic, as they may be short changing your pet. There is the possibility that eventually it will cost you more due to improper diagnosis, treatment, etc. If you are selecting a new veterinarian, feel free to ask for a tour of the clinic. You should inquire about making

an appointment for a tour since all clinics are working clinics, and therefore may not be available all day for sightseers. You may worry less if you see where your pet will be spending the day if he ever needs to be hospitalized.

THE PHYSICAL EXAM

Your veterinarian will check your pet's overall condition, which includes listening to the heart; checking the respiration; feeling the abdomen, muscles and joints; checking the mouth, which includes the gum color and signs of gum disease along with plaque buildup; checking the ears for signs of an infection or ear mites; examining the eyes; and, last but not least, checking the condition of the skin and coat.

He should ask you questions regarding your pet's eating and elimination habits and invite you to relay your questions. It is a good idea to prepare a list so as not to forget anything. He should discuss the proper diet and the quantity to be fed. If this should differ from your breeder's recommendation, then you should convey to him the breeder's choice and see if he approves. If he recommends changing the diet, then this should be done over a few days so as not to cause a gastrointestinal upset. It is customary to take in a fresh stool sample (just a small amount) for a test for intestinal parasites. It must be fresh, preferably within 12 hours, since the eggs hatch quickly and after hatching will not be observed under the microscope. If your pet isn't obliging then, usually the technician can take one in the clinic.

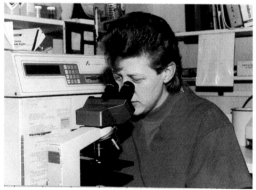

Most lab tests are performed right in your own veterinarian's office and results are usually made available on the same day.

IMMUNIZATIONS

It is important that you take your puppy/dog's vaccination record with you on your first visit. In case of a puppy, presumably the breeder has seen to the vaccinations up to the time you acquired custody. Veterinarians differ in their vaccination protocol. It is not unusual for your puppy to have received vaccinations for distemper, hepatitis,

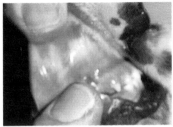

To test capillary refill time, press your thumb against the gum (the gum will be white), and then count the amount of time it takes to gain color back.

It is a good idea to routinely x-ray the chest and abdomen on any dog hit by a car.

leptospirosis, parvovirus and parainfluenza every two to three weeks from the age of five or six weeks. Usually this is a combined injection and is typically called the DHLPP. The DHLPP is given through at least 12 to 14 weeks of age, and it is customary to continue

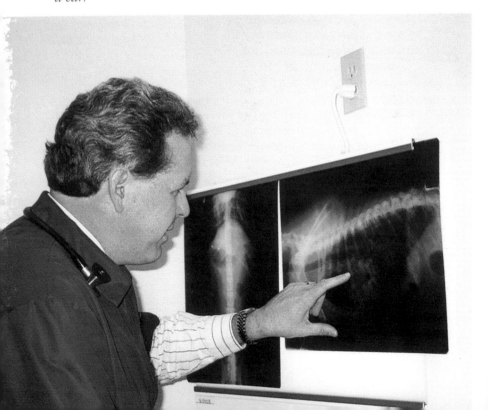

with another parvovirus vaccine at 16 to 18 weeks. You may wonder why so many immunizations are necessary. No one knows for sure when the puppy's maternal antibodies are gone, although it is customarily accepted that distemper antibodies are gone by 12 weeks. Usually parvovirus antibodies are gone by 16 to 18 weeks of age. However, it is possible for the maternal antibodies to be gone at a much earlier age or even a later age. Therefore immunizations are started at an early age. The vaccine will not give immunity as long as there are maternal antibodies.

Puppies cannot be handled by strangers until they have received all their shots. This series is usually completed between the 8th to 12th week of life.

The rabies vaccination is given at three or six months of age depending on your local laws. A vaccine for bordetella (kennel cough) is advisable and can be given anytime from the age of five weeks. The coronavirus is not commonly given unless there is a problem locally. The Lyme vaccine is necessary in endemic areas. Lyme disease has been reported in 47 states.

Distemper

This is virtually an incurable disease. If the dog recovers, he is subject to severe nervous disorders. The virus attacks every tissue in the body and resembles a bad cold with a fever. It can cause a runny nose and eyes and cause gastrointestinal disorders, including a poor appetite, vomiting and diarrhea. The virus is carried by raccoons, foxes, wolves, mink and other dogs. Unvaccinated youngsters and senior citizens are very susceptible. This is still a common disease.

Hepatitis

This is a virus that is most serious in very young dogs. It is spread by contact with an infected animal or its stool or urine. The virus affects the liver and kidneys and is characterized by high fever, depression and lack of appetite. Recovered animals may be afflicted with chronic illnesses.

Leptospirosis

Once you acquire your Dalmatian puppy you should take him to a veterinarian.

This is a bacterial disease transmitted by contact with the urine of an infected dog, rat or other wildlife. It produces severe symptoms of fever, depression, jaundice and internal bleeding and was

fatal before the vaccine was developed. Recovered dogs can be carriers, and the disease can be transmitted from dogs to humans.

Parvovirus

This was first noted in the late 1970s and is still a fatal disease. However, with proper vaccinations, early diagnosis and prompt treatment, it is a manageable disease. It attacks the bone marrow and intestinal tract. The symptoms include depression, loss of appetite, vomiting, diarrhea and collapse. Immediate medical attention is of the essence.

Rabies

This is shed in the saliva and is carried by raccoons, skunks, foxes, other dogs and cats. It attacks nerve tissue, resulting in paralysis and death. Rabies can be transmitted to people and is virtually always fatal. This disease is reappearing in the suburbs.

Any change in the activity level or appearance of your dog at any age should be cause for concern. You should study your dog's daily habits to know when something is amiss.

Bordetella (Kennel Cough)

The symptoms are coughing, sneezing, hacking and retching accompanied by nasal discharge usually lasting from a few days to several weeks. There are several disease-producing organisms responsible for this disease. The present vaccines are helpful but do not protect for all the strains. It usually is not life threatening but in some instances it can progress to a serious bronchopneumonia. The disease is highly contagious. The vaccination should be given routinely for dogs that come in contact with other dogs, such as through boarding, training class or visits to the groomer.

Coronavirus

This is usually self limiting and not life threatening. It was first noted in the late '70s about a year before parvovirus. The virus produces a yellow/brown stool and there may be depression, vomiting and diarrhea.

Lyme Disease

Lyme disease is contracted from the tiny deer tick. Always check your Dal for ticks as soon as he comes in from the outdoors.

This was first diagnosed in the United States in 1976 in Lyme, CT in people who lived in close proximity to the deer tick. Symptoms may include acute lameness, fever, swelling of joints and loss of appetite. Your veterinarian can advise you if you live in an endemic area.

After your puppy has completed his puppy vaccinations, you will continue to booster the DHLPP once a year. It is customary to booster the rabies one year after the first vaccine and then, depending on where you live, it should be boostered every year or every three years. This depends on your local laws. The Lyme and corona vaccines are boostered annually and it is recommended that the bordetella be boostered every six to eight months.

Annual Visit

I would like to impress the importance of the annual check up, which would include the booster vaccinations, check for intestinal parasites and test for heartworm. Today in our very busy world it is rush, rush and see "how much you can get for how little." Unbelievably, some non-veterinary businesses have entered into the vaccination business. More harm than good can come to your dog through improper vaccinations, possibly from inferior vaccines and/or the wrong schedule. More than likely you truly care about your companion dog and over the years you have devoted much time and expense to his well being. Perhaps you are unaware that a vaccination is not just a vaccination. There is more involved. Please, please follow through with regular physical examinations. It is so important for your veterinarian to know your dog and this is especially true during middle age through the geriatric years. More than likely your older dog will require more than one physical a year. The annual physical is good preventive medicine. Through early diagnosis and subsequent treatment your dog can maintain a longer and better quality of life.

This is Ixodes scapularis, *the deer tick. Courtesy of Virbac Laboratories, Inc., Fort Worth , Texas.*

Intestinal Parasites

Hookworms

These are an almost microscopic intestinal worms that can cause anemia and therefore serious problems, including death, in young puppies. Hookworms can be transmitted to humans through penetration of the skin. Puppies may be born with them.

Roundworms

These are spaghetti-like worms that can cause a potbellied appearance and dull coat along with more severe symptoms, such as vomiting, diarrhea and coughing. Puppies acquire these while in the mother's uterus and through lactation.

Both hookworms and roundworms may be acquired through ingestion.

Whipworms

These have a three-month life cycle and are not acquired through the dam. They cause intermittent diarrhea usually with mucus. Whipworms are possibly the most difficult worm to eradicate. Their eggs are very resistant to most environmental factors and can last for years until the proper conditions enable them to mature. Whipworms are seldom seen in the stool.

Intestinal parasites are more prevalent in some areas than others. Climate, soil and contamination are big factors contributing to the incidence of intestinal parasites. Eggs are passed in the stool, lay on the ground and then become infective in a certain number of days. Each of the above worms has a different life cycle. Your best chance of becoming and remaining worm-free is to always pooper-scoop your yard. A fenced-in yard keeps stray dogs out, which is certainly helpful.

I would recommend having a fecal examination on your dog twice a year or more often if there is a problem. If your dog has a positive fecal sample, then he will be given the appropriate medication and you will be asked to bring back another stool sample in a certain period of time (depending on the type of worm) and then be rewormed. This process goes on until he has at least two negative samples. The different types of worms require different medications. You will be wasting your money and doing your dog an injustice by buying over-the-counter medication without first consulting your veterinarian.

Whipworms are hard to find unless one strains the feces, and this is best left to a veterinarian. Pictured here are adult whipworms.

OTHER INTERNAL PARASITES

Coccidiosis and Giardiasis

These protozoal infections usually affect puppies, especially in places where large numbers of puppies are brought together. Older dogs may harbor these infections but do not show signs unless they are stressed. Symptoms include diarrhea, weight loss and lack of appetite. These infections are not always apparent in the fecal examination.

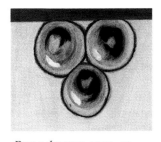

Roundworm eggs, as would be seen on a fecal evaluation. The eggs must develop for at least 12 days before they are infective.

Tapeworms

Seldom apparent on fecal floatation, they are diagnosed frequently as rice-like segments around the dog's anus and the base of the tail. Tapeworms are long, flat and ribbon like, sometimes several feet in length, and made up of many segments about five-eighths of an inch long. The two most common types of tapeworms found in the dog are:

Hookworms, close-up showing teeth.

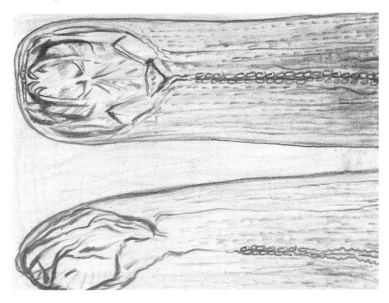

(1) First the larval form of the flea tapeworm parasite must mature in an intermediate host, the flea, before it can become infective. Your dog acquires this by ingesting the flea through licking and chewing.

(2) Rabbits, rodents and certain large game animals serve as intermediate hosts for other species of tapeworms. If your dog should eat one of these infected hosts, then he can acquire tapeworms.

HEARTWORM DISEASE

This is a worm that resides in the heart and adjacent blood vessels of the lung that produces microfilaria, which circulate in the bloodstream. It is possible for a dog to be infected with any number of worms from one to a hundred that can be 6 to 14 inches long. It is a life-threatening disease, expensive to treat and easily prevented. Depending on where you live, your veterinarian may recommend a preventive year-round and either an annual or semiannual blood test. The most common preventive is given once a month.

Fleas can be very problematic to exterminate. Not only does the dog need to be treated, but everything in his environment—his bed, his kennel, your home, etc.

EXTERNAL PARASITES

Fleas

These pests are not only the dog's worst enemy but also enemy to the owner's pocketbook. Preventing is less expensive than treating, but regardless I think we'd prefer to spend our money elsewhere. I would guess that the majority of our dogs are allergic to the bite of a flea, and in many cases it only takes one flea bite. The protein in the flea's saliva is the culprit. Allergic dogs

The cat flea is the most common flea of both dogs and cats.

have a reaction, which usually results in a "hot spot." More than likely such a reaction will involve a trip to the veterinarian for treatment. Yes, prevention is less expensive. Fortunately today there are several good products available.

If there is a flea infestation, no one product is going to correct the problem. Not only will the dog require treatment so will the environment. In general flea collars are not very effective although there is now available an "egg" collar that will kill the eggs on the dog. Dips are the most economical but they are messy. There are some effective shampoos and treatments available through pet shops and veterinarians. An oral tablet arrived on the American market in 1995 and was popular in Europe the previous year. It sterilizes the female flea but will not kill adult fleas. Therefore the tablet, which is given monthly, will decrease the flea population but is not a "cure-all." Those dogs that suffer from flea-bite allergy will still be subjected to the bite of the flea. Another popular parasiticide is permethrin, which is applied to the back of the dog in one or two places depending on the dog's weight. This product works as a repellent causing the flea to get "hot feet" and jump off. Do not confuse this product with some of the organophosphates that are also applied to the dog's back.

Some products are not usable on young puppies. Treating fleas should be done under your veterinarian's guidance. Frequently it is necessary to combine products and the layman does not have the knowledge regarding possible toxicities. It is hard to believe but there are a few dogs that do have a natural resistance to fleas. Nevertheless it would be wise to treat all pets at the same time. Don't forget your cats. Cats just love to prowl the neighborhood and consequently return with unwanted guests.

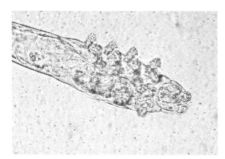

On animals that are born with defective immune. systems the number of demodex mites can increase and cause problems.

Adult fleas live on the dog but their eggs drop off the dog into the environment. There they go through four larval stages before reaching adulthood, and thereby are able to jump back on the poor unsuspecting dog. The cycle resumes and takes between 21 to 28 days under ideal conditions. There are environmental products available that will kill both the adult fleas and the larvae.

Ticks

Ticks carry Rocky Mountain Spotted Fever, Lyme disease and can cause tick paralysis. They should be removed with tweezers, trying to pull out the head. The jaws carry disease. There is a tick preventive collar that does an excellent job. The ticks automatically back out on those dogs wearing collars.

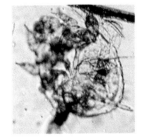

A sarcoptic mite is the culprit of "scabies." This is probably the itchiest condition that affects dogs.

Sarcoptic Mange

This is a mite that is difficult to find on skin scrapings. The pinnal reflex is a good indicator of this disease. Rub the ends of the pinna (ear) together and the dog will start scratching with his foot. Sarcoptes are highly contagious to other dogs and to humans although they do not live long on humans. They cause intense itching.

Demodectic Mange

This is a mite that is passed from the dam to her puppies. It affects youngsters age three to ten months. Diagnosis is confirmed by skin scraping. Small areas of alopecia around the eyes, lips and/or forelegs become visible. There is little itching unless there is a secondary bacterial infection. Some breeds are afflicted more than others.

Cheyletiella

This causes intense itching and is diagnosed by skin scraping. It lives in the outer layers of the skin of dogs, cats, rabbits and humans. Yellow-gray scales may be found on the back and the rump, top of the head and the nose.

DENTAL CARE for Your Dog's Life

So you've got a new puppy! You also have a new set of puppy teeth in your household. Anyone who has ever raised a puppy is abundantly aware of these new teeth. Your puppy will chew anything it can reach, chase your shoelaces, and play "tear the rag" with any piece of clothing it can find. When puppies are newly born, they have no teeth. At about four weeks of age, puppies of most breeds begin to develop their deciduous or baby teeth. They begin eating semi-solid food, fighting and biting with their litter mates, and learning discipline from their mother. As their new teeth come in, they inflict more pain on their mother's breasts, so her feeding sessions become less frequent and shorter. By six or eight weeks, the mother will start growling to warn her pups when they are fighting too roughly or hurting her as they nurse too much with their new teeth.

Puppies need to chew. Nylabones® satisfy this need. Be sure to supply your puppy with plenty of Nylabone® products so that it does not begin chewing on your furniture or other dangerous (and valuable) items.

Puppies need to chew. It is a necessary part of their physical and mental development. They develop muscles and necessary life skills as they drag objects around, fight over possession, and vocalize alerts and warnings. Puppies chew on things to explore their world. They are using their sense of taste to determine what is food and what is not. How else can they tell an electrical cord from a lizard? At about four months of age, most puppies begin shedding their baby teeth. Often these teeth need some help to come out and make way for the permanent teeth. The incisors (front teeth) will be replaced first. Then, the adult canine or fang teeth erupt. When the baby tooth is not shed before the permanent tooth comes in, veterinarians call it a retained deciduous tooth. This condition will often cause gum infections by trapping hair and debris between the permanent tooth and the retained baby tooth. Nylafloss® is an excellent device for puppies to use. They can toss it, drag it, and chew on the many surfaces it presents. The baby teeth can catch in the nylon material, aiding in their removal. Puppies that have adequate chew toys will have less destructive behavior, develop more physically, and have less chance of retained deciduous teeth.

Dalmatian owners should only use Frisbees® with a dog bone molded on top. This helps the dog get a grip on the Frisbee® if it lands flat on a smooth surface. *The trademark Frisbee is used under license from Mattel, Inc., California, USA.*

During the first year, your dog should be seen by your veterinarian at regular intervals. Your veterinarian will let you know when to bring in your puppy for vaccinations and parasite examinations. At each visit, your veterinarian should inspect the lips, teeth, and mouth as part of a complete physical examination. You should take some part in the maintenance of your dog's oral health. You should examine your dog's mouth weekly throughout his first year to make sure there are no sores, foreign objects, tooth problems, etc. If your dog drools excessively, shakes its head, or has bad breath, consult your veterinarian. By the time your dog is six months old, the permanent teeth are all in and plaque can start to accumulate on the tooth surfaces. This is when your dog needs to develop good dental-care habits to prevent calculus build-up on its teeth. Brushing is best. That is a fact that cannot be denied. However, some dogs do not like their teeth brushed regularly, or you may not be able to accomplish the task. In that case, you should consider a product that will help prevent plaque and calculus build-up.

The Plaque Attackers® and Galileo Bone® are other excellent choices for the first three years of a dog's life. Their shapes make them interesting for the dog. As the dog chews on them, the solid polyurethane massages the gums which improves the blood circulation to the periodontal tissues. Projections on the chew devices increase the surface and are in contact with the tooth for more efficient cleaning. The unique shape and consistency prevent your dog from exerting excessive force on his own teeth or from breaking off pieces of the bone. If your dog is an aggressive chewer or weighs more than 55 pounds (25 kg), you should consider giving him a Nylabone®, the most durable chew product on the market.

The Gumabone®, made by the Nylabone Company, is constructed of strong polyurethane, which is softer than nylon. Less powerful chewers prefer the Gumabones® to the Nylabones®. A super option your dog is the Hercules Bone®, a uniquely shaped bone named after the great Olympian for its exception strength. Like all Nylabone products, they are specially scented to make them attractive to your dog. Ask your veterinarian about these bones and he will validate the good doctor's prescription: Nylabones® not only give your dog a good chewing workout but also help to save your dog's teeth (and even his life, as it protects him from possible fatal periodontal diseases).

Chooz® by Nylabone is an edible, hard treat that is delectable and affordable.

By the time dogs are four years old, 75% of them have periodontal disease. It is the most common infection in dogs. Yearly examinations by your veterinarian are essential to maintaining your dog's good health. If your veterinarian detects periodontal disease, he or she may recommend a prophylactic cleaning. To do a thorough cleaning, it will be necessary to put your dog under anesthesia. With modern gas anesthetics and monitoring equipment, the procedure is pretty safe. Your veterinarian will scale the teeth with an ultrasound scaler or hand instrument. This removes the calculus from the teeth. If there are calculus deposits below the gum line, the

The Gumabone® is made of strong polyurethane and is recommended to those dogs that are less powerful in their chewing habits.

veterinarian will plane the roots to make them smooth. After all of the calculus has been removed, the teeth are polished with pumice in a polishing cup. If any

Hercules® and Nylabone® Tug Toys are excellent for your Dalmatian's teeth and fun too!

medical or surgical treatment is needed, it is done at this time. The final step would be fluoride treatment and your follow-up treatment at home. If the periodontal disease is advanced, the veterinarian may prescribe a mediated mouth rinse or antibiotics for use at home. Make sure your dog has safe, clean and attractive chew toys and treats. Chooz® treats are another way of using a consumable treat to help keep your dog's teeth clean.

Rawhide is the most popular of all materials for a dog to chew. This has never been good news to dog owners, because rawhide is inherently very dangerous for dogs. Thousands of dogs have died from rawhide, having swallowed the hide after it has become soft and mushy, only to cause stomach and intestinal blockage. A new rawhide product on the market has finally solved the problem of rawhide: molded Roar-Hide® from Nylabone. These are composed of processed, cut up, and melted American rawhide injected into your dog's favorite shape: a dog bone. These dog-safe devices smell and taste like rawhide but don't break up. The ridges on the bones help to fight tartar build-up on the teeth and they last ten times longer than the usual rawhide chews.

As your dog ages, professional examination and cleaning should

Molded rawhide, called Roarhide™ by Nylabone®, is very hard and safe for your dog. It is eagerly accepted by Dalmatians.

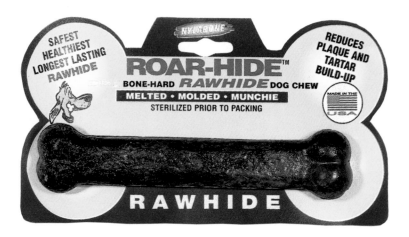

The Gumabone® Plaque Attacker™ is specifically designed for reducing tartar and plaque on your Dalmatian's teeth.

become more frequent. The mouth should be inspected at least once a year. Your veterinarian may recommend visits every six months. In the geriatric patient, organs such as the heart, liver, and kidneys do not function as well as when they were young. Your veterinarian will probably want to test these organs' functions prior to using general anesthesia for dental cleaning. If your dog is a good chewer and you work closely with your veterinarian, your dog can keep all of its teeth all of its life. However, as your dog ages, his sense of smell, sight, and taste will diminish. He may not have the desire to chase, trap or chew his toys. He will also not have the energy to chew for long periods, as arthritis and periodontal disease make chewing painful. This will leave you with more responsibility for keeping his teeth clean and healthy. The dog that would not let you brush his teeth at one year of age, may let you brush his teeth now that he is ten years old.

If you train your dog with good chewing habits as a puppy, he will have healthier teeth throughout his life.

IDENTIFICATION and Finding the Lost Dog

There are several ways of identifying your dog. The old standby is a collar with dog license, rabies, and ID tags. Unfortunately collars have a way of being separated from the dog and tags fall off. I am not suggesting you shouldn't use a collar and tags. If they stay intact and on the dog, they are the quickest way of identification.

For several years owners have been tattooing their dogs. Some tattoos use a number with a registry. Here lies the problem because there are several

A tall fence is an owner's security that his Dalmatian cannot get loose.

registries to check. If you wish to tattoo, use your social security number. The humane shelters have the means to trace it. It is usually done on the inside of the rear thigh. The area is first shaved and numbed. There is no pain, although a few dogs do not like the buzzing sound. Occasionally tattooing is not legible and needs to be redone.

The newest method of identification is microchipping. The microchip is a computer chip that is no larger than a grain of rice. The veterinarian implants it by injection between the shoulder blades. The dog feels no discomfort. If your dog is

lost and picked up by the humane society, they can trace you by scanning the microchip, which has its own code. Microchip scanners are friendly to other brands of microchips and their registries. The microchip comes with a dog tag saying the dog is microchipped. It is the safest way of identifying your dog.

An identification tag placed on your Dalmatian's collar should carry your address and phone number in case he is ever lost.

FINDING THE LOST DOG

Blending in with his harlequin backdrop, this Dalmatian would be difficult to spot.

I am sure you will agree with me that there would be little worse than losing your dog. Responsible pet owners rarely lose their dogs. They do not let their dogs run free because they don't want harm to come to them. Not only that but in most, if not all, states there is a leash law.

Beware of fenced-in yards. They can be a hazard. Dogs find ways to escape either over or under the fence. Another fast exit is through the gate that perhaps the neighbor's child left unlocked.

Below is a list that hopefully will be of help to you if you need it. Remember don't give up, keep looking. Your dog is worth your efforts.

1. Contact your neighbors and put flyers with a photo on it in their mailboxes. Information you should include would be the dog's name, breed, sex, color, age, source of identification, when your dog was last seen and where, and your name and phone numbers. It may be helpful to say the dog needs medical care.

Offer a *reward*.

2. Check all local shelters daily. It is also possible for your dog to be picked up away from home and end up in an out-of-the-way shelter. Check these too. Go in person. It is not good enough to call. Most shelters are limited on the time they can hold dogs then they are put up for adoption or euthanized. There is the possibility that your dog will not make it to the shelter for several days. Your dog could have been wandering or someone may have tried to keep him.

3. Notify all local veterinarians. Call and send flyers.

4. Call your breeder. Frequently breeders are contacted when one of their breed is found.

5. Contact the rescue group for your breed.

Should your Dalmatian ever get loose, be sure to post flyers and signs any place that is heavily populated.

6. Contact local schools—children may have seen your dog.

7. Post flyers at the schools, groceries, gas stations, convenience stores, veterinary clinics, groomers and any other place that will allow them.

8. Advertise in the newspaper.

9. Advertise on the radio.

TRAVELING with Your Dog

The earlier you start traveling with your new puppy or dog, the better. He needs to become accustomed to traveling. However, some dogs are nervous riders and become carsick easily. It is helpful if he starts with an empty stomach. Do not despair, as it will go better if you continue taking him with you on short fun rides. How would you feel if every time you rode in the car you stopped at the doctor's for an injection? You would soon dread that nasty car. Older dogs that tend to get carsick may have more of a problem adjusting to traveling. Those dogs that are having a serious problem may benefit from some medication prescribed by the veterinarian.

Do give your dog a chance to relieve himself before getting into the car. It is a good idea to be prepared for a clean up with a leash, paper towels, bag and terry cloth towel.

The safest place for your dog is in a crate, although close confinement can promote carsickness in some dogs. If your dog is nervous you can try letting him ride on the seat next to you or in someone's lap.

An alternative to the crate would be to use a car harness made for dogs and/or a safety strap attached to the harness or collar. Whatever you do, do not let your dog ride in the back of a pickup truck unless he is securely tied on a very short lead. I've seen trucks stop quickly and, even though the dog was tied, it fell out and was dragged.

I do occasionally let my dogs ride loose with me because I really enjoy their companionship, but in all honesty they are safer in their crates. I have a friend whose van rolled in an accident but his dogs, in their fiberglass crates, were not injured nor did they escape. Another advantage of the crate is that it is a safe place to leave him if you need to run into the store. Otherwise you wouldn't be able to leave the windows down. Keep in mind that while many dogs are overly protective in their crates, this may not be enough to deter dognappers. In some states it is against the law to leave a dog in the car unattended.

Never leave a dog loose in the car wearing a collar and leash. I have known more than one dog that has killed himself by hanging. Do not let him put his head out an open window. Foreign debris can be blown into his eyes. When leaving your dog unattended in a car, consider the temperature. It can take less than five minutes to reach temperatures over 100 degrees.

TRIPS

Perhaps you are taking a trip. Give consideration to what is best for your dog—traveling with you or boarding. When traveling by car, van or motor home, you need to think ahead about locking your vehicle. In all probability you have many valuables in the car and do not wish to leave it unlocked. Perhaps most valuable and not replaceable is your dog.

Pet seats are designed to protect your dog from injury by securing him in place and preventing him from disturbing driver and passengers. Photo courtesy of Four Paws.

Give thought to securing your vehicle and providing adequate ventilation for him. Another consideration for you when traveling with your dog is medical problems that may arise and little inconveniences, such as exposure to external parasites. Some areas of the country are quite flea infested. You may want to carry flea spray with you. This is even a good idea when staying in motels. Quite possibly you are not the only occupant of the room.

Unbelievably many motels and even hotels do allow canine guests, even some very first-class ones. Gaines Pet Foods Corporation publishes *Touring With Towser*, a directory of domestic hotels and motels that accommodate

Crates are the best way to ensure that your Dalmatian is safe during a car ride. guests with dogs. Their address is Gaines TWT, PO Box 5700, Kankakee, IL, 60902. I would recommend you call ahead to any motel that you may be considering and see if they accept pets.

Sometimes it is necessary to pay a deposit against room damage. Of course you are more likely to gain accommodations for a small dog than a large dog. Also the management feels reassured when you mention that your dog will be crated. Since my dogs tend to bark when I leave the room, I leave the TV on nearly full blast to deaden the noises outside that tend to encourage my dogs to bark. If you do travel with your dog, take along plenty of baggies so that you can clean up after him. When we all do our share in cleaning up, we make it possible for motels to continue accepting our pets. As a matter of fact, you should practice cleaning up everywhere you take your dog.

Depending on where your are traveling, you may need an up-to-date health certificate issued by your veterinarian. It is good policy to take along your dog's medical information, which would include the name, address and phone number of your veterinarian, vaccination record, rabies certificate, and any medication he is taking.

AIR TRAVEL

When traveling by air, you need to contact the airlines to check their policy. Usually you have to make arrangements up to a couple of weeks in advance for traveling with your dog. The airlines require your dog to travel in an airline approved fiberglass crate. Usually these can be purchased through the airlines but they are also readily available in most pet-supply stores. If your dog is not accustomed to a crate, then it is a good idea to get him acclimated to it before your trip. The day of the actual trip you should withhold water about one hour ahead of departure and no food for about 12 hours. The airlines generally have temperature restrictions, which do not allow pets to travel if it is either too cold or too hot. Frequently these restrictions are based on the temperatures at the departure and

Ventilation during travel is a most important consideration.

arrival airports. It's best to inquire about a health certificate. These usually need to be issued within ten days of departure. You should arrange for non-stop, direct flights and if a commuter plane should be involved, check to see if it will carry dogs. Some don't. The Humane Society of the United States has put together a tip sheet for airline traveling. You can receive a copy by sending a self-addressed stamped envelope to:

Humane Society of the United States
Tip Sheet
2100 L Street NW
Washington, DC 20037.

Regulations differ for traveling outside of the country and are sometimes changed without notice. Well in advance you need to write or call the appropriate consulate or agricultural department for instructions. Some countries have lengthy quarantines (six months), and countries differ in their rabies vaccination requirements. For instance, it may have to be given at least 30 days ahead of your departure.

Do not allow your pet Dalmatian to ride in the car with its head out the window. Foreign objects can easily enter the eyes or mouth, and he may become injured at sudden stops.

Do make sure your dog is wearing proper identification. You never know when you might be in an accident and separated from your dog. Or your dog could be frightened and somehow manage to escape and run away. When I travel, my dogs wear collars with engraved nameplates with my name, phone number and city.

Another suggestion would be to carry in-case-of-emergency instructions. These would include the address and phone number of a relative or friend, your veterinarian's name, address and phone number, and your dog's medical information.

BOARDING KENNELS

Perhaps you have decided that you need to board your dog. Your veterinarian can recommend a good boarding facility or possibly a pet sitter that will come to your house. It is customary for the boarding kennel to ask for proof of vaccination for the DHLPP, rabies and bordetella

Boarding kennels are safe and provide your dog with the company of other pets. vaccine. The bordetella should have been given within six months of boarding. This is for your protection. If they do not ask for this proof I would not board at their kennel. Ask about flea control. Those dogs that suffer flea-bite allergy can get in trouble at a boarding kennel. Unfortunately boarding kennels are limited on how much they are able to do.

For more information on pet sitting, contact NAPPS: National Association of Professional Pet Sitters
1200 G Street, NW
Suite 760
Washington, DC 20005.

Our clinic has technicians that pet sit and technicians that board clinic patients in their homes. This may be an alternative for you. Ask your veterinarian if they have an employee that can help you. There is a definite advantage of having a technician care for your dog, especially if your dog is on medication or is a senior citizen.

You can write for a copy of *Traveling With Your Pet* from ASPCA, Education Department, 441 E. 92nd Street, New York, NY 10128.

SUGGESTED READING

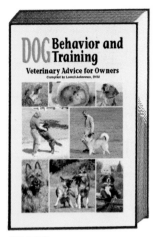

TS-252
*Dog Behavior and
Training*

TS-249
*Skin & Coat Care for
Your Dog*

TS-214
*Owner's Guide to
Dog Health*

TS-205
*Successful Dog
Training*

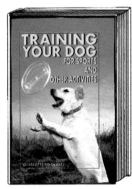

TS-258
*Training Your Dog
For Sports and Other
Activities*

TW-137
*Proper
Care of
the
Dalmatian*

PS-823
*The
Dalmatian*

INDEX